From Mafalda
to Los Supermachos

FROM MAFALDA TO LOS SUPERMACHOS

Latin American Graphic Humor as Popular Culture

DAVID WILLIAM FOSTER

LYNNE RIENNER PUBLISHERS • BOULDER & LONDON

Chapter 1 is based on "Cultura popular y lenguas modernas," *Lenguas modernas* 7. Universidad de Chile 7 (1980) 17-20.

An earlier version of Chapter 2 appeared as "Semiological Perspectives in the Study of Latin American Popular Culture, *Eutopías* 1, no. 3 (1985) 113-138.

Chapter 3 appeared in a briefer form in the *Latin American Digest* 15, nos. 3-4 (1981) 1-3, 27.

An earlier version of Chapter 4 was published in Spanish as "Guachomanía y guachofobia en *Las aventuras de Indoro Pereyra* de Roberto Fontanarrosa," *La palabra y el hombre* 36. Universidad Veracruzana, Mexico (1980) 12-22. It was also included in Rose S. Minc, ed. *Literature and Popular Culture in the Hispanic World: A Symposium.* Upper Montclair, NJ: Montclair State College (1981) 109-131.

Chapter 5 is based on "Mafalda: An Argentine Comic Strip," *Journal of Popular Culture* 4 (1980) 497-508.

An earlier version of Chapter 7 appeared in Spanish as "Las puertitas del Sr. López," *La palabra y el hombre* 44. Universidad Veracruzana, Mexico (1982) 45-55.

Chapter 8 is based on "On the Study of Popular Culture in Latin America," which was included in C. Gail Gunterman, ed., *Contemporary Latin American Culture: Unity and Diversity.* Tempe: Arizona State University, Center for Latin American Studies (1984) 27-43.

Published in the United States of America in 1989 by
Lynne Rienner Publishers, Inc.
1800 30th Street, Boulder, Colorado 80301

and in the United Kingdom by
Lynne Rienner Publishers, Inc.
3 Henrietta Street, Covent Garden, London WC2E 8LU

Library of Congress Cataloging-in-Publication Data

Foster, David William.
　From Mafalda to Los Supermachos.
　Bibliography: p.
　Includes index.
　1. Comic books, strips, etc.—Latin America—History
and criticism. 2. Latin America—Popular culture.
I. Title.
PN6790.L29F67　1989　741.5'098　　　88-32490
ISBN 1-55587-141-0 (alk. paper)

British Cataloguing in Publication Data
A Cataloguing in Publication record for this book
is available from the British Library

Printed and bound in the United States of America

The paper used in this publication meets the requirements of
the American National Standard for Permanence of Paper for
Printed Library Materials Z39.48-1984

Contents

Preface

The analyses of Latin American graphic humor in this book have as their goal the exemplification of an important segment of Latin American popular culture. Although one can easily point to examples of cartoon art and humorous drawings that reveal the strong influence of North American models, there can be little question that there is considerable creative originality among Latin American artists working in both genres. Argentines have been particularly active in this regard, as the research of Trillo and Saccomanno (1981) has demonstrated. Others, Mexicans and Brazilians among them, have also made notable contributions, and artists such as Rius (Eduardo del Río) of Mexico have attained international recognition.

My objective in this book—beyond my conviction that the artists' work deserves the attention of the scholarly community in both Latin American studies and graphic art—has been to promote analysis of a segment of creative popular art. Students of Latin American culture typically acquire familiarity with works that are produced under the aegis of the conventions of high culture or that have been assimilated to the latter (e.g., the Mexican postrevolutionary murals of Rivera, Orozco, or Siquieros), and they thus tend to learn about only a limited range of literary production as representative of the most laudable artistic accomplishments of Latin America. My intention is to awaken an interest in Latin American materials as a whole and to stimulate complementary research.

1

On the Study of
Popular Culture in Latin America

One of the axioms of the contemporary study of foreign cultures is the need to consider an adequate range of representative materials. Thus, it becomes no longer adequate to restrict the study of a foreign culture to the so-called high or elite manifestations. It may remain true that the greatest creative efforts are expended on such phenomena as symphonic music, gallery art, little-magazine poetry, experimental theater, and the like. Nevertheless, the fact remains that, for a majority of Western societies, mass culture forms prevail as not only the most accessible and consumed forms of art, but also the most sociologically typical. The gradual erosion of folk art in the modern world, its assimilation by high art since romanticism, and the emergence of an extensive industry based on the production, promotion, and distribution of mass culture have meant that the latter has perforce become an inescapable ingredient in any comprehensive examination of a nation's culture.

Even when a study aspires, as does this one, to go beyond the strictly routine forms of mass, commercial culture, to study those varieties of popular materials that strive to bring to their composition the creative goals of high culture—often in an attempt to "reform" degrading commercial cultures and bring the modalities of elite works closer to the people—the simple fact remains that we are dealing with a spectrum of materials rarely accorded attention in academic curricula. This has been even truer in foreign language studies, where the study of culture has invariably meant the study of literary classics. In recent years, other cultural modes, such as film,

1

have been included.   But few programs include any formal representation of the extensive array of mass and popular cultural genres, whether in their strictly commercial manifestations or in the more creative efforts examined in this book.

By popular culture we mean all those cultural forms that impinge on our daily lives: newspapers, magazines, movies, television, greeting cards, even phatic speech and social rituals. These phenomena may have a remote folkloric origin and enjoy varying degrees of authenticity to the extent that they spring from profoundly felt popular concerns that are often at extreme variance with an ideologized official image of society. Academe, often an official or semiofficial arm of a ministry of education, is likely to defend the importance of a prize-winning novelist, but society at large is likely not to pay much attention and to go on watching soap operas and sitcoms and reading *fotonovelas* (at least in Latin America).   For better or worse, the citizenry at large perceives—or has been led to perceive—that such forms correspond more closely to the uncertainties and problems of their own existence.

It is not necessary for us to rehearse here the many and complex meanings of folklore, popular culture, official culture, and academic culture (*Hochkultur* or high culture) in an industrialized Western society. Suffice it to say that, though all of these cultural strata support and influence each other, official culture—the "zero" point that prioritizes and promotes different elements and combinations according to prevailing policies—undoubtedly has the greatest prestige.   But it is popular culture that dominates virtually all classes, and, whether or not we find this circumstance reproachable, it is an undeniable sociological fact that cannot help but influence our study of a culture.

One may say bluntly that popular culture has an overwhelming impact on all facets of our daily lives, something that culture merchants know very well how to maximize.   Popular culture sells, a fact readily ascertainable at any newsstand and in any bookstore, record store, TV program guide, or entertainment supplement.   Why then the still modest interest in popular culture in academic sectors, among scholars in either our own or foreign cultures?   In part, it is a question of subtle and unconscious mechanisms that disparage mass forms, a negation that both bespeaks elitist "sophistication" and repudiates the extensive commercialization of the kitschiest forms of popular culture.   Also at issue is the decline of folklore values in the capitalist era, when everything lends itself to a business transaction.

At the same time, it is important to bear in mind that the relative lack of specific density of the products of popular culture (too "easily" understood and consumed), their low degree of symbolic ambiguity and high degree of referentiality, their assembly-line production (such that one work is almost indistinguishable from another), along with various thematic, stylistic, rhetorical, and structural features, all combine to convince us that such artifacts do not deserve analysis. Rather, they seem to lend themselves to little more than content summary and the description of obvious, superficial features.

Yet, research in the field of sociology has demonstrated how incorrect the idea is that popular culture does not lend itself to rigorous scientific examination, and it now becomes the responsibility of those in the humanities who work with foreign cultures to understand how these phenomena, which assume concrete forms ("texts" in the broadest sense of the word) as well as the less tangible forms of customs and social practices, bear as directly on an adequate image of a culture as do the prestige examples more frequently studied.

What are some of the ways to achieve the integration of popular culture studies? There are three typical avenues of inquiry that may serve as illustrations of possible approaches: (1) linguistic phenomena that have a direct relationship with popular culture; (2) verbal texts that constitute "discourses"—in the sense of highly organized artistic or semiartistic texts—taken from the area of popular culture; and (3) texts in which the verbal or linguistic aspect is but one of a range of communicational codes—e.g., soap operas or musical spectacles or sports events—within an overall context based on popular culture patterns.

The conservatism of Spanish lexicography is legendary; it is a quality that extends to other levels of linguistic research—e.g., phonology or syntax—to such an extent that we may discern in Spain and, by extension, Latin America, various reactions to the tripartite motto of the Royal Academy: "Limpia, fija y da esplendor." Consider, for example, the project for a *Diccionario de la real calle española* and the famed *Diccionario secreto* assembled by Camilo José Cela (who is a member of the Royal Academy and a Spanish national senator). It should be obvious that such compilations are rich thesauri of popular culture materials. Cela's *izas, rabizas y colipoterras* (categories of prostitutes), with the wide range of low-class life styles they epitomize, have a secure place in his research compilations, along with an entire alternate image of official Spanish culture. From Cela's lexicographic work to the study of syntax is a modest transition, though it is a necessary one in order to go beyond the mere anecdotal cataloging of nonstandard usage.

There is growing interest in studying features of Latin American Spanish that fall outside the pale of standard academic descriptions, and I could include here some of my own work in this regard as one type of linguistic popular culture. For example, the pattern of exocentric noun-compounding in Argentine Spanish depends heavily on colloquial, ironic, and humorous language. (By an exocentric noun compound, we mean one in which a noun phrase consists of a base noun that is modified, in an adjectival sense, by another noun, rather than by an adjective or adjectival phrase). Spanish, like other Romance languages, does not permit exocentric noun-compounding to the degree that it is a customary pattern in the Germanic languages. Many of the exocentric nouns used in Spanish are calques from scientific or technological terms of English: *año luz* ("light year"), *hora pico* ("peak hour"), *reunión cumbre* ("summit meeting").

Of particular interest for popular culture studies are the many such combinations that represent a form of facetious or ironic naming: *hombre orquesta* ("jack-of-all-trades"), *día sandwich* or *día puente* ("lame-duck day"), *hombre masa* ("mass man"). Studies on linguistic taboos in Mexico, the *albur* (heavy-handed punning), quasi-pornographic rhetoric (A. Jiménez's *Picardía mexicana*), and the language of adolescents contribute to our knowledge of not only one of the richest Latin American dialects, but also one of the most creative in the area of "academically marginal" materials. Promoting an awareness of popular sociodialects and language phenomena that underlie popular culture is an undertaking of undeniable ideological significance, one that cannot be conducted with neutral, scientific objectivity. But there can be no doubt that there are vast areas of Latin American Spanish that transcend academic restrictions and bespeak eloquently the features and criteria of popular culture.

If colloquial linguistic registers are to be found in social communication—"natural discourses"—they may be studied also in terms of their structural substance and how they obey laws governing the composition of speech. Such research, in which the predominant imperative is to uncover the mechanisms that make speech effective and efficient as a symbolic act, may be extended to popular culture phenomena as part of an attempt to analyze "poetic" or "fictitious" discourse. Such discourse exists in texts that have aesthetic pretensions and are acts of communication only in a secondary sense (in the sense of the hypothesis that poetic discourse is not essentially referential when compared to natural and written nonimaginative discourse). Poetic texts ("poetic" in the broadest etymological sense of the word) nevertheless do conform to the norms and restrictions of natural texts or deviate from them in an explicit fashion as part of their metaphoric, ambiguous, defamiliarizing nature.

Although popular culture texts may appear to be natural discourse, they are in reality unquestionably fictitious constructs, and it behooves us to study the tension underlying their linguistic and literary structure, occasioned by the ambiguity or "duplicity" of their frequent attempt to seem nonliterary and documentary. Art is not life, though it often intends to be taken as such. The interest of such works can lie, therefore, in the complex strategies they use to give the impression that they are "nothing but life itself," while being in fact the result of intensive artistic production. This is the case with sitcoms, soap operas, *fotonovelas*, and many movies: They aspire to be taken as life, not imaginative fictions. Television commercials, for example, are notorious for their clumsy—if not downright bad-faith—imitations of natural discourse. But between true natural discourse and the fictitious devices for "naturalizing" advertising, there lies a fertile field of research in terms of linguistic patterns, speech norms, and literary structures. Popular songs also pretend to be natural monologs or diatribes. If one accepts the injunction to "go beyond the sentence" in order to study the pragmatics of linguistic structures, the texts of popular culture are, within the spectrum of fictitious discourses, particularly exemplary, perhaps even more so than those of high literature.

Comic book materials, for example, fall into several fairly discrete categories. On the one hand are those works in which a very simple story line is repeated over and over again in rather obvious and trite combinations. This is the case of the Chilean *Condorito* comics. Other texts deal with common and typical social types—often middle-class families—and, though they may be based on universal models and not represent much artistic or narrative originality, are at least useful for transparent information about life and customs. *Anteojito, Zipi y Zape, Lily, Hermelinda linda, Mortadelo,* and *La abeja Maya* are some examples of this type. Finally, series such as the Mexican *Los Supermachos, Los agachados,* and the materials in the Argentine *Humor registrado* and *Superhumor* magazines constitute, more properly speaking, attempts at creative originality in the graphic arts.

Finally, popular culture phenomena, in contrast to literature or the "practical" registers of business and technology, belong to symbolic processes that extend far beyond the simply verbal. A soap opera is, in addition to dialog, a theatrical spectacle that brings together a range of diverse codes of meaning. Even popular songs that we are accustomed to hearing as merely the combination of words and music are a spectacle where the language of the physical, corporal, even sexual presence of the singer and the accompanying musicians interplays with the strictly linguistic message to produce complex cultural texts. It is in these phenomena, particularly in those popular culture texts elaborated with a high degree of creativity and originality, where language may come close to acquiring the substantial texture characteristic of high literature.

The academic study of popular culture is an intellectual challenge to the extent that it invites us to transcend the compartmentalization of traditional disciplines and to consider, first, that mass culture obeys principles of discourse composition and is, therefore, an appropriate object for the structural analysis of culture; and, second, that popular cultural modalities may serve as the basis for truly innovative artistic texts that go far beyond hackneyed commercial products.

2

Principles of Text Production

 Superficially, it could appear oxymoronic to conjoin the study of Latin American popular culture and the theoretical principles of semiology—that is, the study of the processes by which texts create meaning, their structural organization, and their production within the context of the cultural and ideological codes of a society. Nevertheless, such scholars as Eco (1977) have demonstrated how much we can say about the texts of mass culture by utilizing these principles (and, for the moment, I am using "mass" culture and "popular" culture synonymously, though I will later wish to suggest some distinction between them). But the vast majority of writing about Latin American popular culture has been based on the techniques of content analysis and on a form of ideological interpretation that is one variety of the hermeneutics of meaning in the service of sociocultural analysis. The position papers of Kress, "Structuralism and Popular Culture" (1976), and Hodge, "Linguistics and Popular Culture" (1976) have, with their skeptical conclusions, done little to support a different opinion.

Thus, the bulk of the essays that have appeared in the premier

---

Quoted material from Spanish- and Portuguese-language sources has been translated throughout by the author.

issues of *Studies in Latin American Popular Culture* fulfil essentially the imperative to identify and describe the varieties of mass culture in Latin America, to characterize the themes of these manifestations, and to relate them, if only by implication, to the transnational enterprise of commercial culture for mass consumption. Although the journal's editors encourage a variety of methodological approaches, the comprehensiveness of their coverage and their interest in discovering all the "details" of the industry lead inevitably to essays that are more sociological in focus than oriented toward the ideological and structural principles of text production, more concerned with content analysis and extrinsic features than with the examination of the processes of meaning. *Studies* is fulfilling an important role in the academic study of a major area of Latin American culture, which has too long been ignored or disdained. But its primary emphasis sustains, if only unintentionally, the remoteness of analytical perspectives for an approach to the subject.

Dorfman's approach to popular culture analysis, set out in his enormously influential studies, is even more persuasive in this regard. In his essays on the impact of U.S. comic books in Latin America (1972, 1974, 1983) and in his interpretations of how the racist and classist ideologies of these materials condition a certain manner of understanding their own culture by Third World readers, Dorfman has provided impressive instruments for one form of the ideological interpretation of culture in Latin America. Yet these essays are essentially content analyses, though they do imply a form of reader-response criticism. It is clear that for Dorfman and those scholars who have followed his lead (Herner, Amorós, Alvarez Constantino), the principles of meaning in the Disney studios or Marvel comic books derive from relatively easily identifiable themes (that appear to us to be ridiculously blatant once we have had them called to our attention). As a consequence, Dorfman's writings persuade us that they deal with a clear and evident reality, with, in short, an unequivocal and directly recoverable meaning that is much more inviting to metacommentary enthusiasm than the subtle—arcane?—scholia of Eco. That Latin American scholars tend to agree on the urgency of adequate cultural interpretations for dependent societies only serves to enhance the appeal of a writing that is predicated on the axiom of transparent content on which attention only need be focused in a sustained fashion.

But even such analyses contain the fertile seeds of a more extensive analysis of the principles of text production. Having suggested the contrary goals of content analysis, I now must recognize how such instruments can, in fact, lead naturally into a study that satisfies the theoretical demand to examine the principles of meaning rather than its transtextual reformulation into successive thematic interpretations, or as corollaries to texts serving quite different discourse goals (i.e., the reading of mass culture texts to confirm another text's formulation of specific sociopolitical goals: Implicit in Dorfman's analysis is the need to discredit Donald Duck or Superman comic books because of the negative self-image they promote in the Third World reader).

As a consequence, I would like to explore here the possibilities inherent in some of the model analyses of Hispanic popular culture materials for the articulation of an investigation based on the structural and rhetorical principles of text production.

For example, Herner's ambitious survey (1979) of Mexican *fotonovelas* and comic books contains an exceptionally interesting—and unannounced—change of focus when it moves from providing statistical information about these publications in Mexico and the details of the vast and cynically operated industry to a fascinating but frustratingly brief discussion of the language of the comic books and the general configurations of their narrative plotting. Although Herner, a sociologist, would certainly question the suggestion of a semiological approach for her discussion, I would like to insist that her interest at this point in her exposition deals precisely with important aspects of these texts that are related to the production of meaning.

However, these two portions of Herner's study are particularly suggestive to the extent that they imply a sense of the status of the object as text (this is especially so in the case of graphic language, as a consequence of the awareness of how the verbal language and graphic conventions are coordinated into a single, continuous whole to be grasped by the reader) and of the way in which entire groups of texts—specific series or specific genres of materials—are underlain by narrative programs in the sense of a specific nucleus of plot possibilities.

Thus, "The balloon is one of the basic elements of the specific language of the comic strip. There exists a great variety of those elements that fulfil different functions: They express states of mind, setting, and thoughts" (p. 44). Herner goes on to provide examples of "when someone yells," "when someone dreams," "when someone speaks on the radio or television." The illustration of almost a dozen such examples is followed by a sampling of onomatopoeias. Herner observes (p. 53):

> Onomatopoeias serve the function of clarifying the action that is
> taking place. They do so in two ways. One is through a graphic or
> plastic representation, determined by the space the balloon
> occupies within the frame, its size, form, color, and so on. The
> other is acoustic, which involves translating sound into image.

This observation is important in that these details involve the
explicit coordination of the verbal text and the graphic image into
one meaningful textual unit.

In the case of the observation about plot nuclei, Herner (p. 265)
also demonstrates an awareness of how texts are structured as
discourse events in which the role of the receptor-reader is encoded
into the artistically communicative act:

> Our role as readers lies in suffering with the actors and imagining
> their future happiness as best we can, since happiness as a theme
> is not marketable. Also not on sale are daily life and much less-
> amorous intimacy. However, we have already seen why moral
> values are: They are the epilog of every comic book on sale.
> Everything, or almost everything, can be portrayed, but in the end
> what triumphs is the sacred conventional morality that sustains our
> world. Adultery brings death; feminine infidelity is in particular
> unpardonable. Prostitution is ill-advised . . . in the end, and
> crime does not pay, unless the assassin is a mass-media hero,
> Pinochet's fascist army, or the police: They believe they have the
> right to kill. It does not matter whether *sins* are paid for on earth
> or in heaven, but rather the fact that you understand you cannot
> go against the established order because you will be punished.
> Once you know this, do what you want, and if you cannot, read
> about it in the pages of comic books, with the advantage that
> punishment occurs there and redeems you at the same time.

One will note how this statement is three-pronged, with a triple
insinuation of analytical concerns. In the first place, Herner
addresses an unspecified *usted* that is the implied—and
ideal—reader of the text (and in the case of this section of her
analysis, it is a matter of para- or pseudopornographic *fotonovelas*).
The expectations of the sociocultural code of this reader is an
integral part of the textual strategies. In the second place, there is a
very clear sense of narrative program, of a particular sort of plot
trajectory involving verificational consequences (i.e., given certain
circumstances, certain things are about to happen: Adultery will
necessarily lead to punishment). At another point in the same
general discussion, Herner speaks of "sex instead of . . ." (pp.
266ff.), in which the disingenuous morality of the *fotonovelas* masks
forms of pornography and its typical plot configurations. Whether or

not one subscribes to the Propp-Greimas-Todorov concept of narrative programs, schemas, typologies, and trajectories, the important point is that Herner accepts the idea that narrative texts are underlain by discernible sorts of plot structure, that this structure has a certain abstractness about it that constitutes a common base for groups of narratives, and that this structure in some way corresponds to patterns of cause-and-effect that we may contemplate in the events of everyday life and in our interpretation of them in moral and other terms.

The discussion, in turn, of pseudopornography and of narrative schemas that involve culturally bound plot possibilities (i.e., once again, if you commit adultery, you will be punished; or if you cheat a sainted little old lady of her nest egg, a superhero like Kalimán will get you) allows Herner to underscore how such texts enjoy an intertextuality with the narrative programs attributable to everyday life. Since Herner decries the cynical exploitativeness of Mexican *fotonovelas*, she does not see this relationship in the positive terms a literary scholar might in describing how novels or dramas give a heightened reformulation of the sociocultural texts or "natural" narrative possibilities by which we live.

Rather, Herner's concern is with how the *fotonovela* disingenuously distorts the narrative programs of the social text, and how it plays cynically on their most repressive aspects in order to justify their alleged or putative moral value. And this, of course, opens up the possibility of a comparative analysis of the ideologemes, in Jameson's (1981) terminology, of this form of mass popular culture and alternatively socially committed forms (some of which I will comment on below). Jameson (p. 87) defines ideologeme as:

> an amphibious formation, whose essential structural characteristics may be described as its possibility to manifest itself either as a pseudoidea—a conceptual or belief system, an abstract value, an opinion or prejudice—or as a protonarrative, a kind of ultimate class fantasy about the "collective characters" which are the class in opposition.

The possibilities of applying such a formulation to the comparative analysis of the material Herner examines and of other artistic texts, "popular" or otherwise, should be obvious. (A comparative examination is implied by Herner's harsh assessment of the texts she examines, in view of the critic's knowledge that alternate, more socially redeeming versions of these narrative programs exist.)

Sempere, in his path-breaking study, *Semiología del infortunio,* summarizes as follows one aspect of his investigation (p. 166):

> The *fotonovela*, like the comic, undergoes an iconic aberration
> in the *asynchrony* imposed by the need to represent in a single
> vignette the visual equivalent of verbal discourse.
>
> Dialog is temporal and successive, and at times it is even
> simultaneous, when there are three people who converse in a
> single frame. Nevertheless, visual representation is singular. It
> represents a unique, *selected* moment of verbal discourse.
>
> Language in the *fotonovela* must resolve this semiological
> conflict by creating the conventional figure of *asynchrony*. That is
> to say, it not only resolves it, but it takes it as its own.
>
> In *asynchronic* representations, each character freezes his
> gesture or bodily expression at the most meaningful moment of
> his respective discourse.

Up to a certain point, this is a valid observation on Sempere's
part, though it is unquestionably the same point to be made about
any narrative trajectory represented in graphic terms, including the
most socially prestigious forms of visual art like, say, religious
paintings portraying narrative events with or without accompanying
legends. Nevertheless, it is clear that Sempere strives for the
definition of a salient aspect of the principles of textual organization
and meaning production in the material he is examining. Not
differing substantially from Herner in his metacritical ideology—he
too decries the cynical or exploitative distortion of reality to be
found in the series of Spanish *fotonovelas* he examines (*Lucecita*
and *Simplemente María*)—Sempere focuses on language and
ideology through an examination of the general configurations of
plot. Representative sections include "New and Old Archetypes,"
"Content and Ideology," "Analysis of Content and Represented
Values," "Situation Units," and "The Suffering of the Triangle."

Despite its title, however, Sempere's investigation rarely
accomplishes more than does Herner's straightforward content
analysis. In the first place, there is something of a hypallage or
catachresis about the conjunction *semiología del infortunio*.
Sempere—and, presumably, no other researcher—is really interested
in the real-life phenomena lumped together under the heading
"misfortune." Of course, there is a logical structure in the events of
daily life, and the logical structures of narratives enjoy a certain
degree of symmetrical relationship with the former (and the outlines
of narrative typologies must, therefore, constitute an abstract
mediation between the two). But Sempere does not undertake the
investigation of the structure of real-life misfortunes, in the fashion

of one type of research interest in the structure of possible events and actions and their relationship to discourse representations (e.g., Dijk 1980). Sempere's concern is with a form of popular culture narrative texts and their organizational principles in conformance with an ideology of the artistic representation of misfortune, its salient features and the establishment of a commercially successful appeal to the emotional needs of ideal readers. But Sempere's title seems to imply that his interest lies with an examination of the semiology of the transtextual content of *fotonovelas* rather than with the specific strategies of meaning of these products toward discerning underlying ideological and narrative principles. The latter is what the reader extracts from his book, its title notwithstanding.

The second problem with Sempere's research is that, despite all of the suggestive headings, it does not in the final analysis rise much above content analysis. It is not that one demands a Todorovian grammatical analysis of plot situations: This would only confirm what any reader already knows, to wit that there is a numbing monotony about the plot possibilities of *fotonovelas* (or soap operas and any other similar form of mass popular narrative). Rather, the problem lies with a tendency to engage in content analysis and not to carry through with relating that analysis to any sustained discussion of the organizational principles of the texts. Thus, the foergoing quotation is about the best I can do to find in Sempere's book a representative example of the sort of thing I feel can be said about popular cultural materials from a semiological—whether proto or actual—point of view.

One misses relating the specific point about asynchrony, which is a valid one that explains one aspect of the stiff artificiality of the putatively "realistic" photography that characterizes the *fotonovelas*, to further observations about the overall compositional features of the individual frames, their successive relationship to each other, and the homologous relationship between the attitudes struck by the actors in the photographic frames and the accompanying verbal text. A favorite illustrative example is the conjunction of a pose showing someone answering a telephone (an important figure of modern communication in texts relating problems of amorous interpersonal communication) and an accompanying legend that says "X answers the telephone." This is a form of narrative redundancy that is only qualitatively different from the redundancy of any meaningful strategy in narrative texts, such as a narrative action undertaken successfully several times to make a thematic "point" to the reader, or a narrative action explained from several different perspectives in order to highlight it as a constituent in the narrative trajectory.

Yet Sempere is not constrained to go into this question in any detail with the essential features he identifies, and the result is a superficiality that is a long way from satisfying the demand to work in detail with representative texts, such that characteristics identified and conclusions drawn have the greatest implications possible for a wide range of phenomena. Since we cannot examine every text in depth—because of their sheer number and because we work, in the case of mass, commercial, popular culture, with the axiom that there is little substantive difference between the texts of a "genre" that would justify examining each of thousands of, say, *fotonovelas* in detail—it is exceedingly important that any investigation of the salient features be as detailed as possible. Aside from arguing the artistic bankruptcy and the exploitative ideology of the *fotonovelas*, Sempere does not provide very much generalizable analysis that his reader can extend to other products. Herner's comments on onomatopoeic language are, in the end, more generalizable than any of Sempere's points; see also Gubern (1972) on the language of comic books.

Much more satisfying as a specifically narratological analysis is Amorós's essay, "Corín Tellado: quince fotonovelas completas, seleccionadas entre las mejores," from his *Subliteraturas* (1974). Although Amorós is not explicitly interested, in his book, in either structural or semiological analyses, what he does end up providing in the longest essay of his study (in which the other entries are very straightforward discussions of content and meaning) is an account of the underlying narrative principles of a group of Corín Tellado's famous texts. (Amorós's study is not, however, the most suggestive essay on Corín Tellado. Any discussion of the Corín Tellado phenomenon must begin with Cabrera Infante's perceptive commentary on the inherent and unstinting pornography of these works, a commentary that can be turned to more analytical ends through a specific consideration of the extensional meanings of signifiers that make an ostensible claim to be dealing with "romantic" love, but which really suggest a conjunction of meaning in the domain of proscribed erotic passion.)

However, returning to Amorós's more staidly academic investigation, the critic is able to distill from the study of fifteen representative texts a number of basic narrative patterns that he then characterizes for their variants and interrelationships. The following sort of synthetic characterization (p. 158) is typical of the implica-

tions to be drawn from his analysis, since the principle of retardation is a significant aspect of narrative organization:

> The entire development of the *fotonovela* can be defined as a way
> (more or less successful, depending on the case) to retard the
> happy ending that has been completely foreseen from the
> beginning. On occasion, the clash between two temperaments, or
> sentimental indecision is enough to accomplish this. At other
> times, a rival (man or woman) fulfils the structural function of
> creating a conflict that the reader, no matter how unperceptive,
> perceives as nonexistent. It is reasonable for it to be a jealous rival
> who creates obstacles or who bribes an old boyfriend of the girl to
> return and awaken great confusion in her.

Our ability to foresee the outcome of a narrative trajectory is
part of the pleasure we derive from reading texts (i.e., the
satisfaction of our ability to interpret adequately the signposts of
foreshadowing and of our familiarity with possible narrative
grammars). By the same token, retardation, as a part of the
controlling ecphrasis of the text ordained by the practical
consideration of length or by the artistic one of appropriately
significant exposition, is what permits the trajectory to end "before
its time." In this way, retardation is what accounts for the recursions,
reversals, inversions, and various other recastings of the structural
elements that keep the plot going. We are well aware of how, in the
soap opera and other kinds of serial literature, episodes that end in
cliffhangers and other sudden crises fulfil a guiding principle of
retardation.

Like other materials examined so far, Amorós's comments are
more informed by the same sort of intuition about the nature of
texts that underlies semiological analyses, without presence of the
scientific metalanguage that characterizes the latter. Nevertheless, it
is clear that what the critic is providing is essentially the
representation of the principles of meaning underlying a group of
texts rather than simply a series of plot summaries. Characteristically
repetitive in the nature of the themes and situations with which they
deal, *fotonovelas* do nonetheless reveal the bulk of the features of
literature and natural narratives that discourse analysis has focused
on (see Pratt especially in this regard). There is no reason why a
more explicit analysis of Corín Tellado's production and other
materials cannot satisfy our curiosity as to how, given the
overwhelming repetitiveness of content, these texts are able to
manipulate various narrative schemes in order to provide some
semblance of distinctive difference from one example to another

while maintaining a rigorous uniformity of ideology, point of view, and verbal and visual styles.

The coeditor of *Studies in Latin American Popular Culture*, Hinds, exemplifies in his published research on Mexican comic books the basic interest of *Studies* in content analysis and extrinsic, contextualizing information. Yet once again, we are able to discern in his work conclusions that have interesting implications for a discussion of text production. Hinds (1977) examines Mexico's answer to Superman, *Kalimán: el hombre increíble*. The critic provides the usual sort of information one expects to find in these studies: data concerning the creation and distribution of the stories, as well as statistics about sales and readership; the general thematic configurations of the various issues, including overlapping with other publications and echoes of foreign strips; the fundamental ideology to be derived from the sorts of actions portrayed, their trajectory and resolution; and the interaction between the hero and supporting characters and antiheroes.

For example, Hinds observes that "Kalimán serves to exemplify the nonsexual aspect of the Mexican macho, representing an asceptic macho" and that "Kalimán is the model of Mexican honor" (p. 43), a circumstance that explains much of the comic's enormous popularity in Mexico as the glorification of stereotypic images of a national ethos. Kalimán appeals to positive Mexican self-images and represents a national model to counter the foreign one of, to use Dorfman's phrase, *Superman y sus amigos del alma*. However, as a commercial, mass cultural product, *Kalimán* does not go beyond the conventions of the Superman genre.

At one point, Hinds (p. 38) summarizes a typical plot configuration in the Kalimán narratives. I find of particular interest his emphasis on the figurativization of the thematic conflict:

> In a typical plot, Kalimán battles a formidable variety of diabolical characters and revolting animals. The principal villains are somewhat different from the group that supports them. The former are generally greedy and cruel men, scientists obsessed with controlling the world, or dishonorable persons who seek revenge against their enemies at any cost. The sordid characters of lesser importance tend to reflect fears more than unfulfilled dreams. Our childish phobias about rats, spiders, serpents, bats, wasps, leeches, and other specimens are constantly magnified. For example, Kalimán is attacked by some giant poisonous spiders, by mountains of tarantulas, by legions of snakes, monstrous crocodiles, and venomous and carnivorous wasps. Dangerous enemies are found in the form of humanized plants like, for

example, animals and semihumans, and carnivorous plants with flesh and human emotions.

Aside from whatever interest these details may provide in terms of Barthian cultural codes, or myths and archetypes formulatable in psychoanalytic terms, or simply traditional Good-Evil symbolizations, the principal interest to be pursued from Hinds' comments would concern the patterns of figurativization to be found in a popular culture series like *Kalimán*. That is: How, precisely, do the recurring narrative conflicts become embodied in specific clusters of verbal images? How are these images part of the interplay between pseudoreality and the grotesque visual hyperbole of a certain kind of comic strip? Clearly, *Kalimán* is in the tradition of the grotesque types in *Dick Tracy*, the Marvel comics (e.g., Rubberman and company or Batman's adversaries), and lurid forms of science-fiction fantasy, where the visual texture involves the interplay between almost recognizable quotidian reality and the gross figures of the contest between Good and Evil.

Greimas and Courtès (1982) use the term figurativization to refer to the embodiment of abstract narrative primes into the fictionally "real" figures of time, space, and character. This is what should also be of interest in the analysis of the specific representations of narrative schemes in popular cultural narratives. However, it is also necessary, in the case of graphic narratives, to understand the term as referring to both verbal and visual features of the texts, with the latter playing the far greater role: The *arañas venenosas* are more likely to be developed in the narrative through visual images than they are to be described in the accompanying texts. Hinds does not distinguish between the verbal and the visual in *Kalimán*, but his comments provide us with an important point of departure for an investigation of this important Mexican work.

If *Kalimán* is a true-blood Mexican answer to Superman, *El Payo* fulfils the archetypic role of the Lone Ranger. In another study, Hinds (1982) discusses this equally successful strip, which has the added interest of a main character who mediates between the myths of the Mexican Revolution and the political realities of the institutionalized system. This ideological aspect of the strip should merit extensive examination in terms of how it is given a semantic configuration through the use of event, action, and characters, since so much contemporary Mexican culture, "high" or otherwise, is concerned with the same chasm between the myth and the reality of the revolution, and it is therefore undoubtedly one of the main attractions of *El Payo* for its reading public.

However, Hinds chooses not to develop this possibility, contenting himself with the usual exposition of extrinsic features of the strip and general comments on the main outlines of the plot configurations. In the more explicit terms of narrative principles, these configurations could be reformulated so as to bring out the structural relations between characters, between main plot line and subplots, and to justify the choice of plots in terms of El Payo's role as a mediator between exploiters and exploited, a force that is able to violate given semantic categories by ameliorating the lot of the latter to the disadvantage of the former. Hinds' comments (p. 41) on the plots of the strip, however, only obliquely suggest such an approach:

> The plots of *El Payo* are unusually intricate, and like many of the elements in the comic book, they have been carried out progressively throughout the years. Besides the incessant struggle between the Panaderos and the Pesqueiras, there are endless minor plots, several of which a specific issue will develop. Other villains with goals similar to those of the Pesqueiras are confronted and finally defeated; human beings communicate with the spiritual world; and a host of characters who covet wealth, Juan José, or Lupe. Much of the action centers on an apparently interminable struggle of the Panaderos to reunite their nuclear family, since often one of the parents or one of the children has momentarily fallen into the hands of some villain. Finally, many of the characters are not static, but rather change and develop over time. Juan José, for example, marries and raises a family.

Up to this point, I have been using the terms "mass" and "popular" culture interchangeably. Certainly, none of the examples of actual texts would require any subtlety of terminology, and it is likely that few of the researchers whose analyses I have discussed read these texts with the pleasure associated with so-called high culture literature and graphic art. As necessary as it may be to question the prevailing distinctions between high culture and various gradations of "lesser" art, Amorós's blunt denomination, *subliteraturas*, does not seem to be really deplorable as a characterization of the texts he examines.

Of greater urgency, however, is the recognition that, in contemporary culture—especially in Latin America—there is a form of truly creative, innovative, probing artistic expression that pursues the traditional if somewhat vague goals of high culture while employing many of the techniques, strategies, and materials of mass, commercial culture. In the case of novelistic works, the examples are well known: the Argentine Manuel Puig's novels, for example, which assume the disguises of pulp fiction, or many of the works of the novelists of *La Onda* in Mexico, science fiction in Brazil, the soap opera pre-texts of the Peruvian Mario Vargas Llosa's *La tía Julia y el escribidor*. In the case of graphic art, the Mexican Rius (see Tatum and Hinds 1979; Speck 1982) and the Peruvian Juan Acevedo are producing comic books that certainly have a quite different sociopolitical objective than do the materials studied by Dorfman. Argentina's Quino (Joaquín Salvador Lavado) has been extensively studied as a truly original creative force (see "Mafalda . . . ," Koch 1981). Argentina is particularly endowed with gifted artists of this nature (see Trillo and Saccomanno 1981; Steimberg 1977).

I would like to close the present discussion of the ways in which an analysis of the principles of text production may contribute to an adequate critical discussion of popular culture, whether mass-commercial or sociopolitically committed, by characterizing the disjunctive textual strategies of the Brazilian Ziraldo in his *Jeremias, o Bom* strip, one of his major artistic efforts (see Cirne 1973).

The most important aspect of *Jeremias, o Bom* is the fact that it was published at a time—1969—when there was virtually no extensive or adequate social commentary in Brazil. *Jeremias* was published barely five years after the April 1, 1964, military coup. The actual strips were, of course, drawn at a date even closer to this watershed in recent Brazilian sociopolitical history. In the editorial cartoons that Ziraldo draws at the present time for the editorial page of the prestigious *Jornal do Brasil*, he takes to task some of the pretensions of the current government of Brazil, as well as commenting acerbically on the military governments of some of Brazil's neighbors, such as Argentina and Chile. But by contrast, the material published in *Jeremias, o Bom* is relatively restrained in its form of social commentary.

Yet perhaps the best way of approaching the sort of social criticism that Ziraldo engages in is in terms of a very critical, albeit urbanely humorous, representation of certain social and cultural values, certain national tics of the Brazilian people that are themselves metonymic indexes of underlying and fundamental social problems, which a reader able to "read" the implied social text appropriately will comprehend.

The dominant focus of *Jeremias, o Bom* is on the relationship between the central figure as an archetypic embodiment of self-sacrifice, disinterested generosity, passive acceptance of the conflicts and tensions of his society, and the members at large (so to speak) of the community with which he comes in daily contact. The disjunctive texture of the panels derives from the fact that the elements that Jeremias interacts with—aggressiveness of his fellow men, the insouciant irresponsibility of his brethren, and so on—are all in stark contrast to his own gentle and rueful manner. For example, in one panel we see Jeremias's interaction with a crowd of people attempting to squeeze into an elevator (see Plate 2.2). In the face of the problem—that there is room for only one more person—Jeremias is willing to yield his place to the frantic individual who arrives just as he is about to enter the full car. It is significant to note that, in addition to the way in which the line of waiting passengers is a virtual anthology of social types, Jeremias is distinguished from them by the distinctive device of the solid black appearance of his own image in contrast to the white outlined in black of the others. In this sense, it is especially clear that we are to understand a relationship of Jeremias versus the others.

Since Ziraldo's drawings are organized in terms of the disjunction, Jeremias versus the others, it is necessary to examine in detail how the panels foreground Jeremias and the strategies for making him the focal point of a form of social commentary. Even though the strips are not photographically realistic but rather make use of bold strokes and general line configurations, the context in which Jeremias appears is relatively proportional and realistic in terms of the general features of the individuals, event, or action portrayed. Within that context, the figure of Jeremias is both simplistic and grotesque. This detail underscores the dominant characteristic of identifying Jeremias—identifying him in the graphic sense of pinpointing him in each drawing—in his representation as solidly black.

In the cover drawing (Plate 2.1) there are a number of features of grotesque exaggeration: Jeremias is portrayed as having no trunk to his body, and there is nothing below the waist but his spindly legs and enormous shoes; the shoulder area is extremely accentuated and schematic, especially with the geometric centering of the tie; the man wears an old-fashioned stiff collar, and the lines on his face suggest a more or less constant state of abashment. The disconsonance of the figure of Jeremias in terms of the other more relatively realistically represented characters is one of Ziraldo's strategies for establishing a focal point of reference for Jeremias. Another of the strategies for identifying a disjunction between the protagonist and the other figures in the strip is that there is a relative accentuation of movement and action on the part of the other characters.

For example, in one strip involving a soccer game, Jeremias would essentially be lost in the shuffle of his arguing teammates were it not for the fact that his solid black jersey provided him with some sort of distinctive relief. In the first panel he is a focal point of silence amid the shouting discord of the others, whose expressive facial gestures and wildly gesticulating arms suggest the intensity of the disagreement among them. Jeremias attains movement only to impose silence by his outstretched arms and conciliatory words to the similar effect in the final panel; these words are presumably drowned out by the shouts of pleasure from the players, suggested by their posture in the third panel.

One finds in these strips and drawings that Jeremias retains essentially the same posture or physical attitude throughout the successive individual frames, while other characters are represented in various forms of motion—running, bending over, kneeling down, gesturing, shouting, and so on. Jeremias maintains a rigidity of posture around which the others move and gesture. For example, one strip consists of two double-page panels. In one, we see the guests of a very lively party engaged in the characteristically boisterous conversation of such affairs. In the next panel, as we turn the page, we find Jeremias. He lies prone on the floor, covered by equally boisterous children whom he is entertaining while their parents enjoy the party going on in the other room. The two panels are joined by the clever graphic device of having the page, the two sides of which carry half of each panel, serve as the wall between the two rooms. A window between the two rooms allows us to see the festivities in the one room as Jeremias babysits in the other.

In line with the fact that the other characters move and Jeremias remains static—or comparatively static—so are the others endowed with the effusive speech one associates with stereotypic images of Brazilians. The exclamatory statements, the rhetorical intensification of language, the excessive volume and pitch of speech are all features customarily, if not strictly accurately in a sociological sense, attributed to Brazilians as exuberant extroverts, with Rio's fabled *joie de vivre*. By contrast to the effusiveness of his fellow citizens, Jeremias is essentially mute. Moreover, his facial expression—and the lines of his face most likely represent less his need for a shave than they do an embarrassment over the situations in which he finds himself—and his vacant eyes (a graphic way of portraying surprise or wonder) are techniques for endowing him with physical features that set him off from the other individuals.

It is significant to underscore the ironic thrust of Jeremias's name: the prototype of the complainer, the lamenter. However, Ziraldo's Jeremias does not complain nor does he bemoan. Rather, he regrets by implication the behavior of others that he, essentially unconsciously, sets off by his own deportment. This he does by implication because of the lack of demonstrative commentary on his part. His name is semantically explicit as well as ironically inappropriate in terms of his actual confrontation with the behavior of others, which certainly would appear—at least in the world Ziraldo evokes—to merit the critical appraisal of the social commentator.

Such a commentary is, of course, transferred from Jeremias by the artist to the reader capable of assessing the gap between Jeremias and his brethren. Toward this end, one of the most notable devices Ziraldo employs in order to frame Jeremias's behavior and the real-life situations in which our protagonist finds himself is the use of social clichés. Social clichés and the daily circumstances of social intercourse are then inverted or ruptured by Jeremias's inability to accept such circumstances on their own terms, and by his obdurate insistence on behaving in conformance with some other, presumably more noble and therefore outlandish, ideal. For example, in one cartoon the inversion concerns the accepted wisdom that a man who agrees to double-date will end up with the uglier of the two women. But Jeremias's friend, who accepts the blind date, ends up with the attractive and curvaceous cousin, while Jeremias is happy to accompany the singularly uglier of the two women.

Another characteristic of Ziraldo's graphic strategies is the interplay between the grotesque nature of Jeremias's behavior—grotesque because it deviates so radically from a presumed Brazilian informal social norm and because of the artist's very fine costumbristic procedure of focusing on foibles in the Brazilian national character—and the carefree "naturalism" with which the prototypic Brazilians move through the strip. In one double panel (see Plate 2.3), Ziraldo updates the hoary commonplace of the caveman who wins his woman by clubbing her, juxtaposing Jeremias, who will accost her with a bouquet of flowers, with his less poetic fellow men, who await the Ipanemaesque woman with their clubs at the ready.

Finally, the strip is particularly interesting in the way in which the reader is asked to engage in a complicity with Jeremias. Even though the reader is presumably a member of the social community that Ziraldo evokes so humoristically, the individual reader nevertheless is not likely to want to accept the fact that he or she is irresponsible, unthinkingly selfish, or so inattentive to the feelings of others. By focusing graphically on Jeremias and by endowing him in an exaggerated fashion with positive social values in juxtaposition to the appallingly negative social characteristics of the individuals with whom he comes in contact, the strip in essence induces the reader to identify with Jeremias. Such an identification may serve to effect a level of sociocultural "therapy" in terms of the Brazilian character, as though the strip were colored by the overriding rhetorical question, "Wouldn't it be nice if we could all be like Jeremias?" This may not be the stuff of biting social criticism, but Ziraldo has turned it into a highly successful strip, one that is unquestionably indicative of serious cartoon art in Latin America. It is precisely this sort of material about which analyses of the production of cultural texts may be expected to have the most to say.

PLATE 2.1

PLATE 2.2

PLATE 2.3

3

Sábat: Caricature as Cultural De-Kitschification

Hermenegildo Sábat (born in Montevideo, Uruguay, in 1933) has published in a wide variety of sources, but he is best known as the principal editorial cartoonist for the Buenos Aires daily *Clarín*. Although *Clarín* is one of the most outspoken newspapers in Argentina (within, to be sure, the Draconian limits imposed by the recurring military governments of recent decades), the lot of an editorial cartoonist in present-day Argentina is not an easy one. *Seré breve* (1975), a collection of Sábat's interpretations of events during the short-lived resurgence of Peronism, is undoubtedly one of the most important documents of the period.

If Sábat has been successful, it is due less to any scathing interpretation that may be attached discursively to his drawings than it is the result of the fancifulness if not the outright expressionistic quality of his work with the pen: Sábat is a sort of Oliphant without words and definitely without the sarcastic penguin in the corner.

Although Sábat figures prominently for his editorial work, the most creative manifestation of his expressionistic drawings is found in his books on other artists: *Al troesma con cariño* (1971)—easily his most famous work and the one that I will study in detail below—deals with Mr. Tango, Carlos Gardel; *Yo Bix, tú Bix, él Bix* focuses on Leon Bix Beiderbecke, Gardel's contemporary and an

27

equally important musical force in Buenos Aires; *Georgie dear* (1974) is an acerbic interpretation of the literary persona of Jorge Luis Borges. Sábat's two most recent collections concern Aníbal Troilo and Toulouse Lautrec.

Aníbal Troilo, who died in 1975, was one of the last of the virtually mythic tango personalities. His talent lay with the *bandoneón*, a complex miniature accordion, which in the hands of another great artist, Astor Piazzola, has been raised to a symphonic instrument. Troilo was a large man, puffy from alcohol and drugs, and one of his nicknames, El Gordo (The Fat Man), serves, through a colloquial paronomasia, as title of Sábat's drawings, *Dogor* (1979). The combination of Troilo's hefty figure and the relative smallness of his *bandoneón* provides an eloquent contrast for these black and white, highly detailed pen sketches. One plate shows Troilo as an immense Buddha, dominating a neighborhood plaza. The statue is surrounded by a small iron fence and the inhabitants go about their usual Buenos Aires–plaza pursuits; El Gordo's extended *bandoneón* is a broad felt-tip squiggle across his midsection. Another highly significant drawing consists of two juxtaposed images of Troilo, who repeatedly appears with butterfly wings. A smaller image is the young, well-groomed performer, playing with calm control. Alongside him, slightly larger and surrounded by a psychedelic aureola is the seedy, bejowled figure of Troilo possessed by the demons of his music. These drawings, in portraying the artistic genius of a performer like Troilo, underscore Sábat's own genius: the ability to frame a central figure that is almost trite in the artist's original conception (Troilo with the butterfly wings; Borges's toothy frozen smile) with an array of structurally integrated details.

The volume on Lautrec (1980) is in a totally different register, in part because of the use of color (as far as I know this is Sábat's first full-color publication); the volume also includes an essay on Lautrec by the Argentine writer Julio Cortázar. The central feature of these drawings is the almost grotesque contrast between the fully clothed dwarfish figure of Lautrec (in some cases finished off by butterfly wings also) and the fleshy women whose bodies, concealed by yards of Victorian bows and ruffles in Lautrec's own drawings, are revealed in all their carnal abundance by Sábat.

The main conceit of Sábat's evocation is the sexual thralldom in which these women held the artist, without whom, however, they would have been long forgotten. As a consequence, many of the drawings depict Lautrec as a bearded, spectacled, hatted homunculus assuming various postures on the bodies of the women he can fully possess only in his drawings of them. One plate shows him resigned to painting the toenails of a monumental naked foot. In another, he dejectedly contemplates a rope ladder that will lead him to the summit of a formidable breast; the supine woman simply stares off into space. In a third plate, Lautrec is nothing more than a saltshaker on the table of the cafés he haunted. The total image reverses the concept of the artist/creator-in-control-of-his-world in order to stress how all great artists are, in a fundamental sense, possessed by their subjects.

Al troesma con cariño (1971) is a collection of some fifty drawings accompanied by key verses from the tango lyrics popularized by Gardel (see Cantón 1972, for an analysis of the Gardelian tango). Thus, in the first instance there is an interplay between words and images, such that the drawing illustrates the familiar verses and the latter predisposes our interpretation of the drawings and the identification of specific elements in them.   In addition to this interplay between codes of meaning, there is a disjunction or discontinuity in Sábat's artistic goal that is particularly productive in terms of the generalized sociocultural meanings we attach to his drawings.   I refer to the uneasy tension between the tendency to enhance the monumentalized or institutionalized image of Gardel and the tendency to mock—to caricaturize—that image. Sábat speaks in his introduction (p. [7]) of his affection for the entire Gardelian mystique, represented paradigmatically by the annual homage on the date of his accidental and violent death (in a plane crash in Medellín on June 24, 1935), while acknowledging the inherent ridiculousness of the whole business:

> Every year since 1935, the last week of June overwhelms everyone's nostalgia and threatens to challenge the iconoclasm of some: movies are shown in neighborhoods, and the lyrics that the Master sang are reprinted. These works of charity enjoy manifestations of absolute solidarity, or almost. I will avoid impersonal euphemisms by confessing that Gardel's movies and lyrics make me laugh, and quite a bit. If I dragged through this world the shame of having lived and the pain of no longer existing, so much the worse. But I see Gardel acting leaning on a ship's railings, and I laugh. I see him again, awaking with his hair slicked back, flirting with Peggy, Betty, Mary, Julie, and I laugh until my sides split. This is irritating to the true believers, who pay to stimulate their *recherche* of time wasted, exactly on the day that chance would have it that they could see him again. [It should be noted that this passage manifests several clever examples of the accommodation of Gardelian lyrics.]

The Gardelian artifacts (the films, which are only stagy opportunities for Gardel to sing) are ludicrous, and the veneration of an uncritical public is equally ludicrous. Sábat goes on (p. [8]) to speak of the solecisms and anacoluthia in the lyrics, a feature rarely dwelt on by commentators (see Fossati 1980[?]; Naipaul 1980; "Scat . . ."):

> After killing Rancales in *Melodía de arrabal* (in self-defense, of course), his redeemed soul leads him to the virginal, shy little music teacher, just five minutes before the end of the movie. I won't give the ending away: I want to be nice. But I don't laugh over what I can't understand. If the questionable feats of plot or some lyrics make me laugh, when Gardel sings I fall to my knees, kiss his hands, and beg a thousand pardons. A heretic yes, but I'm not yet deaf. Because it's easy to laugh when you read,
>
> > Palermo alone is guilty,
> > his bewitching sand deceived me.
>
> Gardel naturally, perhaps mysteriously, transforms this nonsense, this delirium, into something coherent and sensible. I continue to listen to the record, and my recurring incomprehension persists. Since I am neither a researcher nor a writer, nor do I want to be, and since there are a lot of other things that make me laugh, including what I do, I agree that I want to kill the soul that idiotizes my brain, and I go on. Don't laugh.

There is no question that Carlos Gardel is an Argentine national myth, with the result that there is an immense body of writings devoted to sanctifying his participation in Argentine popular culture (see Ferrer 1970, for example), along with a parallel current of writings that underscore his key function in a complex network of exploitive and opportunistic cultural commercializations of the tango, a phenomenon authentically folkloric in its *Volkspoesie* origins. (For literary, rhetorical analyses of the tango, see, e.g., Villariño 1977 and Foster 1983–1984; for a serious sociological study, see Mafud 1966.) In a general sense, we may say that Sábat's introductory comments define the phenomenon of Gardel as quintessential kitsch: an artistic phenomenon characterized by bad taste because of the displaced or skewed conjunction of its elements, or because of the banal repetitiveness, with little compositional originality, of fossilized patterns obeying commercial rather than "creative" demands (Dorfles 1969a, 1969b). I will have more to say below concerning Sábat's reference to the handful of verbal and visual tropes that characterize the Gardelian industry.

The title of the collection alludes obliquely to the tension between the expected (the monumental) and the rupture (the demythificational interpretation of what is considered sacred): "*al troesma*" is a commonplace, the result of the Lunfardo figure of diction, the *vesre* (=*revés*), which is the reverse arrangement of the consecutive syllables of a word—a sort of Argentine pig Latin (Donni de Mirande 1967). Thus, *troesma* is *maestro*, a reference both to Gardel as musician and to his supremacy in a pantheon of artists.

The second phrase, "*con cariño*," bespeaks, on the other hand, the desire to frame the Gardelian mystique, if not in laudatory or mythifying terms, at least in terms of a personal relationship with a phenomenon from which reasonable aesthetic pleasure is derived. The result, then, is a series of caricatural images of Gardel that, instead of demythifying or debunking the sociocultural patterns he synthesized, serve effectively to "de-kitschify" Gardel. This is accomplished by subjecting the rhetorical formulas of the commercialized phenomenon—the recognizable lyrics and the recurring visual motifs—to an artistically recreative foregrounding whereby they are "dignified" by the cartoonist's compositional originality. It is this creative bricolage, making use of stale tropes and basically kitschy material, that characterizes Sábat's personal, affectionate image of Carlos Gardel and the tango he personified. (Sábat is not alone in using elements of kitsch; see, for example, Masiello 1978.)

Sábat's basic strategy is to recreate a Gardelian persona, a presence that dominates the graphic image and controls the lyrics, which are either uttered by the man or are uttered with reference to him. (In general, the narrator of the tango lyrics, "displayed" by Gardel in person or through his recordings, is also the subject of the lyrics, though often the lyrics may concern a third party or a generalized circumstance; in some instances, there is a reflective contrast between the narrator as he is now and as he was then as a former self or virtually as another individual.) This persona combines the *topoi koini*, the commonplaces, of the Gardelian mystique in new expressionistic combinations, with special reference to either the bust of the man or a full-length portrayal in which the face dominates in a disproportionate if not grotesque foregrounding: The features of the face serve as the compositional axis of the drawings.

Take, for example, the image that appears on both the cover and the title page of *Al troesma* (Plate 3.1). As Sábat notes in his prefatory comments, the brim of Gardel's hat seemed always on the same plane as his crooked smile, and this symmetry provides an element of compositional harmony at eloquent variance with the "irregularities" of the other features: (1) the pronouncedly fleshy mouth, partially open as if in the act of articulating a measure of song; (2) the recessed and shaded, or hooded? eyes—rather than the hat veiling the eyes, the rimmed shadows of the eyes seem to impinge on the contours of the hat so that there is an inverisimilar continuity between the absent details of the eyes and the brim that should shield them but is instead etched by the eyes; (3) the ears, which at their lobes lose the lines suggesting fleshy texture and acquire a sculptured appearance, as though they were earrings (the ring-like appearance is all that is showing for the head's left ear lobe); and (4) the exaggerated asymmetrical crown of the hat, finished off by the disproportionately large band with *its* asymmetrical heart design.

Such graphic features enhance the ludicrousness of the Gardelian image identified in the prolog, as well as mark the highly iconoclastic perspective of the artist toward the kitschy elements, the fossilized tropes, of the repertoire of images that characterize the canonical versions of the monumentalized figure. It is the intertextual juxtaposition between these institutionalized and therefore prosaic images of Gardel and Sábat's idiosyncratic reinterpretation of them that lends his drawings their creative originality: They depend on, "demand," our scandalized recognition of the artist's rupture with the canonical versions and his unorthodox reconstitution of the clichéd commonplaces of the commercialized Gardel.

This circumstance of "scandalized" recognition is especially evident in Sábat's explicit representation of the full erotic implications of the tango. As a concession to prevailing bourgeois morality in "Victorian" Argentina, the tango, as part of the aspiration to respectability necessary for its mass-market commercialization, lost much of its original ribaldry and scatological flavor. Allusion to but not direct representation of eroticism was permitted, and the tango may be said to articulate only tangentially, through carefully chosen metonymic commonplaces, the full range of sexual adventurism inherent in the life patterns it refers to.

Yet, Sábat's illustrations of tango verses—or his suggestions for their full and uncensored comprehension—are as explicit as visual art may be in a "respectable" publication in Argentina: (1) A *corte de manga* becomes a phallic icon on a parallel plane with a woman's outstretched arm pointing toward the man's genitals; the woman's pubic area is crossed out—X marks the spot; (2) a woman kissing Gardel virtually fuses with him, and the sharp outlines of one of her breasts moves toward fitting neatly in the goblet he holds in his hand; (3) illustrating the saccharine verses of "Silencio en la noche," the man kneels before the Barbarella vision of the woman, whose pronounced nipples attract the man's eyes through the brim of his hat; "Eran cinco hermanos" alludes not to the old lady's five lost sons in the original text, but to the phallicized fingers of the hands turned in a supplicating gesture toward the woman's body; (4) The woman's body is a guitar—"Guitarra, guitarra mía" is the accompanying text—which the musician skillfully plays, his hands resting on the sound box of the area below her waist.

Particularly creative in this regard is the drawing accompanying the lines "Tal vez te provoque risa / verme tirao a tus pies" (Plate 3.2). Here the same exaggerated motifs of the singer-narrator's head are repeated, though the pathetic masochism implied by the lyrics is belied by the besotted visage, which seems more grazed by the woman's foot than struck by it in the gesture of humiliation the words insinuate. Particularly notable, especially in contrast to the buffoonish image of the man, is the grotesque representation of the woman: The iron-mask visage of her head—the angular outlines and the eyes behind the slots—is counterbalanced by the full swell of the trunk of her body, encapsulated in the shoe that is central to the masochistic fetish of the man's humiliation. Sábat's drawing underscores the monstrous qualities of the man's sexual thralldom, the degraded face of erotic humiliation only hinted at in the elliptic verses.

On a less threatening note is the drawing accompanying one of the tango lyrics' many allusions to their own status as music: "Bandoneón, / porque ves que estoy triste / y cantar ya no puedo." This "metatextual" feature of the lyrics is routinely accompanied by the sort of anthropomorphization we see in Plate 3.3, and the *bandoneón* is addressed as though it was a human interlocutor and indeed as a fully endowed coparticipant in the musical event: The narrator in essence apologizes to the *bandoneón* for not being able to produce song—i.e., for not being able to work with it. Appropriately, Sábat's drawing captures this hypostasizing of the *bandoneón* and its integral relationship with the singer-narrator by blending Gardel and instrument into one phenomenological image.

It is not a question of seeing Gardel's face through the folds of the *bandoneón*, but rather of the surface of the latter becoming the folds of the man's face, transmitting accurately the grimace of sorrow that bespeaks the "I can't go on" commonplace of the lyrics:

The articulating mouth of the lyrics and the (not really parallel) wind-producing mechanism of the *bandoneón* blend in a way that signifies their interdependent union in the production of music; the foregrounded legs of the musician dangle pigeon-toed as useless appendages to the concentration of musical production in the head of the singer and the "body" of his inseparable instrument.

If anatomical continuity exists here between Gardel and his instrument, as it does between head and hat in the cover illustration, in other drawings such continuity exists between the man and the other main instrument of his lyrical expression, a woman's body (Plate 3.4). In this case, the lyrics, "Del fondo de mi copa / su imagen me obsesiona," are not taken in the commonplace sense to mean that the man sees an image of the woman in the bottom of his glass. Rather, the man's head becomes the vessel that contains the image, the memory, of the woman, parodying the simplistic notions of the human mind as a repository of mental pictures: the cliché and the lyrics are duplicated in the cliché of the drawing. In the process, the bathos of the lyrics is mocked by the typically Gardelian vacant smile and by the woman's singularly unseductive facial expression.

Although superficially Sábat's drawings may seem to be nothing more than innocuous, albeit fanciful illustrations of some key verses from the Gardelian tango, their iconoclasm and scandalous parodying point toward a more creatively artistic purpose. By foregrounding processes of rapture with the banal commonplaces of the Gardelian mystique and by stressing those aspects censored by the canonical images, like the libertine eroticism that can only be the life style of the suggestive allusions, Sábat de-kitschifies the monumentalized Gardel and gives free rein to the artistic originality circumscribed by the commercialization of cultural motifs. The result is an "affectionate" portrait of Gardelian commonplaces that springs naturally from the recovery of a personal and creative relationship with a phenomenon, unfettered by the negatively mediating force of kitsch.

PLATE 3.1

PLATE 3.2

PLATE 3.3

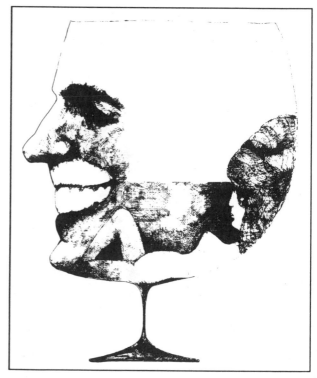

PLATE 3.4

Fontanarrosa's Gauchomania and Gauchophobia in *Las aventuras de Indoro Pereyra*

Roberto Fontanarrosa (born in 1944 in the industrial city of Rosario, Argentina) has been drawing for only a little over a dozen years. Nevertheless, his work has won him a prominent place in contemporary Latin American graphic art (see Rivera 1976a; R. Acosta 1974; Fossati 1980[?]; Trillo and Saccomanno 1981). In addition to his various one-frame or one-strip drawings, represented by the collection *Quién es Fontanarrosa* (1973) and the overwhelming but highly original *Boogie, el aceitoso* (1974–)—one of the strongest images in Latin American popular art of the all-pervasive violence of prevailing imperialistic beliefs—Fontanarrosa is also the creator of that paradigmatic gaucho of the limitless pampas, Inodoro Pereyra, *¡El Renegau!* (1974). Fontanarrosa has published his works with Ediciones de la Flor, a publisher whose list includes, along with "serious" writings of the younger generation of authors, works by the most creative exponents of popular culture in Argentina. What these publications have as their common denominator is the attempt to examine a series of elements from Latin American culture—and specifically from Argentine culture—from a demythifying and denunciatory perspective, with the goal of debunking some of the cherished beliefs of the official, ruling establishment.

In the case of *Las divertidas aventuras de Inodoro Pereyra*, the focus is on the image of the gaucho. There are two elements of Argentine popular culture that have come to serve—and be marketed—as virtual national myths. They are the tango and the gaucho. As happens frequently when phenomena that have authentic popular or folkloric roots are converted into the national myths of a partisan ideology and are subsequently commercialized, kitschification is inevitable (see Dorfles 1969a, 1969b; Méndez 1975). Neither the tango nor the gaucho has been exempt from this process. One of the elements of kitsch in the case of the gaucho is pseudopopular language, an element that is also characteristic of the tango and Lunfardo. If there is a nucleus of sociolinguistic authenticity in kitschified gaucho elements, it is a matter of features that nevertheless are a far cry from any sort of legitimate gaucho speech. If José Hernández's *Martín Fierro*, at least in "La ida" (the first part of the poem published in 1872), was one of the first examples of a counterculture literature in Latin America (Jitrik 1971), its assimilation into the ideology of the myths of an agropecuarian culture and the subsequent commercialization of everything having to do with gauchos exemplify the process by which the poetic is turned into kitsch and the folkloric commercialized.

Thus, Fontanarrosa, seen from the perspective of the commercialization of Argentine national culture, synthesizes the repudiation of one version of cultural shibboleths through the creation of a gauchoesque character who parodies unknowingly (to the extent that there are no indicators of self-reflection on his part) the degradation of the gaucho. In the process, he thus also serves to affirm slyly (since here there are overt signs of an attempt at drawing distinctions) the legendary *viveza criolla* (Creole cleverness). This double characterization is captured by the man's name: If Pereyra is one of the traditional family names to be found in the Argentine countryside, Inodoro (it means "toilet") is nothing less than a heavy-handed allusion to the pretentiousness of certain classic names.

¡El Renegau! is a typical nickname for the rebellious, "renegade" gaucho. Applied to Inodoro Pereyra, it stresses how he is the point of reference for a feeling of rejection toward his society (the orthographic form of the nickname signals the range of details, more ironic than legitimate, that Fontanarrosa uses to suggest rural speech patterns). We can say in general terms that Fontanarrosa undertakes satirically to bring into play some of the hoariest national traditions that have been both mythified and commercialized, ending in perfect examples of rampant kitsch: the clothes, the

gaucho's saddle gear, editions of *Martín Fierro* and Ricardo
Güiraldes's *Don Segundo Sombra* (1926) bound in the leather of an
unborn calf, both the idyllic and the humorous (in the style of
Molina Campos) illustrations of country life, and so on.

The language of Fontanarrosa's *Aventuras* is illustrative of his
satiric goal. It belongs ironically to that tradition of gauchoesque
writings where language is half documentary and half artificial, with
a resulting exploitation of the creative potential of the apparently
verisimilar language of the texts based on the speech patterns of the
gauchos. In the strips, Inodoro Pereyra speaks a language that
aspires to sociolinguistic authenticity, not only in individual words
but also in phonology (represented of course by unconventional
orthography); also to be noted here is Inodoro's diction, both in
popular sayings and metaphorical flourishes. But in contrast to
commercialized phenomena where there is some sort of serious
intent to mirror the gaucho's language (or, at least, those aspects of
it that have assumed the status of a fetish), Fontanarrosa's drawings
employ a series of markers to underline the essential irony of Don
Inodoro's language, as part of the goal to satirize not only the
gaucho but both the gauchophobia and the gauchomania that
prevail in certain sectors of national culture: ". . . e Inodoro
Pereyra, el renegau, se hizo perdiz por los caminos que el viento
traza en la noche. Lejos, el crespin lloraba vaya a saber porqué."
The collection closes with Pereyra's following *envoi*:

> Para quien no guste mi canto
> tengo una cosa prevista
> que se compre una viguela
> o se compre otra revista.

It is evident that this sort of irony promotes a basic ambiguity in
regard to the language of the *Aventuras*, sowing a doubt that is
likely to exist even for many Argentines: What is the demarcation
line between the truly colloquial elements and the distortions by
Fontanarrosa toward debunking the commonplace of gauchomania?
The humorous irony prevailing in the strips consists of using a
legitimate trope in a context where it is out of place (as in the first
example cited above) or of breaking with the unity of the trope (the
case of Pereyra's *envoi*). This irony becomes the dominant
mechanism for laying bare the "eloquent inauthenticity" that colors
the *Aventuras*.

Let us examine, by way of illustration of Fontanarrosa's image of
the gaucho, how the ruptures in the phatic forms of conversation

contribute to the merciless ironizing of the conventional formulas of religion (see Plate 4.1).

While the priest may correctly articulate the conventionalism of first the greeting and then the worn morality he personifies, his speech serves to trigger Don Inodoro's replies, in violation of the tropes' code, by suggesting a double entendre both amusing and defiant. The following presents first what Inodoro actually says, along with the conventional equivalencies that we "read" beneath the text as its ironic counterpoint:

- Sin pecado *conseguida* = concebida: This anticipates the priest's scolding words to Inodoro concerning his immoral, extramarital relations.
- Estoy repasando el *catrecismo* = catecismo: This too is a prefiguration of the erotic theme: *catre* = cama campestre.
- Pecador y guitarrero: The humor lies here in conjoining two elements that do not belong to the same semantic category, thereby suggesting a circumstantial relationship between them.
- le haremos una misa criolla: Creole mass (for example, the famous one by the Fronterizos group) is a folkloric mass with guitars and other popular elements against the grain of the conventionalism the country priest embodies.
- en lugar de sortija yo haría taba o pato: This is yet another example of tying together disparate elements: The marriage ring is taken to be a plaything like the *taba* (roughly, dice) or *pato* (a type of ball with handles).
- Pa[ra] la gracia que tiene vivir ansina: The grace to which the priest alludes has nothing to do with the homophone used by Inodoro and its derived form, *gracioso*.
- No me venga a mentar matriomonios que no conozca: Starting with *mentar*, which implies gossiping, Inodoro takes the metonymic allusion to the Biblical Sodom and Gomorra as the names of couples also living in sin outside the Church.
- Ese pingo es un pingo árabe: In the face of the priest's greed, Inodoro comes up with the hyperbolic pretext that the Arabian horse is an unsuitable donation at a Christian wedding.
- Cruzando pa' la cañada lo pisó un carro: This is a play on words based on *Cruzada*, a fossilized metaphor derived from *cruzar*.

To close the text, the narrator speaks with ruptures that parallel Inodoro's:

- Con una plegaria: There is a play here on the priest's presumed prayer in the face of the sinner's intransigence and thick-headedness, and the bells calling the faithful to prayer, in anticipation of the following joke.
- Era la hora de tomar el tedeum: The strip juxtaposes *tomar el té* and the Te Deum, sung in thanksgiving for an event of great magnitude—the meeting with Inodoro is much more the occasion for wailing and not jubilation for the priest.

In one sense these word plays constitute a series of isolated jokes that are characteristic of Fontanarrosa's strips. But each strip focuses on one distinct but paradigmatic phenomenon concerning the degradation of the gaucho, his commercial mythification within an exploitative ideology, and his cleverness in the face of the values of the dominant society. The jokes serve to reinforce the general pattern of allusions that underlies each one of the illustrated narratives, and they become more important than simply gags designed to ridicule the conventionalism of the priest through their rupture with the commonplaces he embodies.

A great part of the ironic-humoristic play of Fontanarrosa's work derives from *catachresis* and the *spurious neologism*: Either we discover that words are being used incorrectly, with an accompanying distortion or fragmentation of meaning, or if the words do in fact exist in the rural speech of the gaucho, they are nonexistent in the normal lexicon of the educated urban speaker and hence function as though they were neologisms whose meaning is to be deduced broadly from the context in which they appear. Catachresis and spurious neologism—and the unfamiliar (pseudo)archaism—are joined by extravagant pathetic fallacy and a display of fossilized metaphors to make up a completely ridiculous stylistic register. This feature of the strips becomes functionally significant for the ironic role it plays in the characterization of a rural way of life derided and degraded in spite of the vacuous myths of Argentine gauchomania.

The cultural conflict of this degradation is epitomized in the strip dealing with the encounter between Don Inodoro and Charles Darwin, whose comments concerning the inhabitants of the Río de la Plata were far from flattering (Moorehead 1969).

In this case (see Plate 4.2) the play of humorous ruptures does not involve the violation of the conventional formulas of a particular register of Spanish and a catachresis that challenges them, but rather a range of Creole tropes—alternatively the hyperbolic metaphors from the pathetic fallacy of a tattered "poetic" expression and Don

Inodoro's catachresic jokes—versus the paleontologist's appalling Spanish. This disjunction may be seen particularly well in the first frame of the strip, where we move from the hypostatic image of the narrator to Darwin's mangled greeting in "Spanglish": ". . . y el canto que se cantaba / Gud mornin, aparcerou"

This juxtaposition sets in motion a series of semantic conflicts, such that the "conversation" between the two becomes a duet of the deaf, an extravagant clash of linguistic as well as cultural signs (the slanted line marks the break in communication; note also the absurd pictorial metaphor of the narrator in the third frame: "Era una garúa de pecas la mano del gringo"):

- Yon Darwin paleontólogo / Indoro Pereyra, renegau: The two adjectives are not categorically equivalent.
- no haber sentido úste de un gliptodonte / un grito donde: The phonologic deformation stresses the contrast between scientific language and colloquial speech.
- Gliptodonte estar bajo tierra / Deje que le enyene la cueva: At issue here is the ambiguity of "estar bajo tierra."
- animal de la edad de piedra / yo a Piedras no lo conozco mucho: This is an allusion to the metonymic relationship or the antonomasia between the noun *piedra* and the name *Piedras.*
- cientos de años que estar enterrado / ese animal está muerto: At issue here is the ambiguity of *enterrado.*
- no importarme que hacer tanto tiempo muerto / sabía que los gringos comían asquerosidades: Again, there is an ambiguity surrounding "tanto tiempo muerto," which suggests the stereotypes of the foreigner who is considered dirty because he is different (see, for example, Bourke 1891, and Greenblatt 1979).
- yo que ser de la Rubia Albión / Yo soy de la Negra Eulogia: There is also an ambiguity at issue here surrounding the phrase "ser de" in the sense of "venir de" versus "ser de" in the sense of "pertenecer a, ser amante de"; there is also an antinomic relationship between *Rubia* and *Negra.*

Pereyra's "y no digo nada" appears to close off the unsuccessful communication of this "encounter." If the first strip showed the gaucho trumping the priest's expressions of conventional morality, in this strip his words serve to dismiss the presumptuous foreign scientist, for whom Pereyra is nothing more than an "anachoretic gaucho," a not very appropriate description but one nevertheless indicative of the cultural conflict at issue. What is particularly significant is the play based on the feeling of superiority that the gaucho displays toward Darwin: He fails to understand how people could be interested in the things the Englishman inquires about. In the face of the traditional English superiority complex, Don Inodoro's attitude suggests a necessary setting the record straight. In this sense one may see a sustained interplay of cultural concepts, oriented in terms of necessary demythification through the ridicule of commonplaces no longer possessing any kind of symbolic meaning.

The last strip (see Plate 4.3) to be analyzed makes use of the debunking linguistic joke in the context of yet another pattern of ruptures: the "natural," spontaneous, and "poetically" artful speech of the gaucho versus the pretentious and vacuously elegant talk of the pseudogaucho. There can be no doubt that what is at issue is the authentic representative of the gaucho, Don Inodoro Pereyra, versus that bookish defender of Creole customs, Jorge Luis Borges (see, for example, Borges and Casares 1955).

This strip is undoubtedly one of Fontanarrosa's best, as well as one of his most strikingly cruel in its focus on Borges, a figure of Argentina's intellectual elite or aristocracy who, despite his interest in the folk and Creole culture, is considered the antithesis of the "natural" man of the Argentine people. Inodoro Pereyra may well not be precisely the ideal of the noble savage, but neither is Borges seen here as a paragon, and the strip remains bound by an image of cultural authenticity degraded by the senility of the old man and the inconsequentialness of the gaucho's response to him. It is only at the end of the strip that, repudiated by the "perspicacity" of the dog Mendieta, Inodoro's sense of superiority prevails through his prophesy: "yo lo voy a enterrar cuando se muera de viejo."

The strip's irreverence in the face of a monument of Argentine letters is evident in the references to Borges's blindness, his Anglicized nickname, the cadenced periods of his speech along with the characteristic tropes ("en una noche que añoro"), the local-color allusion, his pedantry, the oblique references to ill-willed gossip concerning his sexual underdevelopment, the adherence to outworn sociocultural ideologies (e.g., Domingo Faustino Sarmiento's opposition between "civilización y barbarie"): There can be little doubt that this particular strip demands an extensive familiarity with all that Borges represents as a personality more legendary than historic.

If the strip demands the reader's awareness of a full range of "anecdotal code," it is for the purpose of pursuing a series of oppositions between the two national figures. Once again we may speak of the intersection of commonplaces and misunderstandings that throw into relief both the image of national culture and the repudiation of one of its gauchifying paragons:

- Por favor, señorita / Este ve menos que un gato e yeso: In addition to alluding to Borges' literal blindness, can *ver* mean synonymously *understand* here?
- "Léido" no. "Leído" se dice. Palabra grave / "Facón" es una palabra grave: At issue is the multiple meanings of the word *grave: penultimate stress* versus *weighty.*
- El sol sobre tu frente alumbre tu lenguaje camarada / No soy letrau, sabe?: Aside from the difference in the expressive register, Don Inodoro winds up his declaration with a folk metaphor that subscribes to the antithesis between the "natural" poetry of his speech and the artificiality of his interlocutor's.
- Suelo tener la verba inflamada / ¿y no se pone nada?: The old man's absurd trope is answered by Don Inodoro with a misunderstanding of the meaning of *verba*: He appears to confuse it with *verga = pene.*
- Es inútil, somos un símbolo / Nos desprecea: Borges's rhetorical phrase is identified for what it is—a sense of superiority—by Mendieta, whose rural *desprecea* clashes with it significantly.

If it is possible to reproach Borges for imitating the speech of the gaucho from the bookworm's point of view, Fontanarrosa's cleverness in this strip lies in the imitation of the imitation in a context where it functions as an indicator of one dominant, overwhelming sociocultural position in Argentina.

It would be wrong to speak of Fontanarrosa's *Las aventuras de Inodoro Pereyra* as undertaking the restoration of the romantic image of the gaucho, the portrait of the noble savage that Lugones sought to enshrine in the national epic (1916) (the same one that Borges, speaking of *Martín Fierro*, called the assassin of a novel in verse; 1953, 1965). Yet there is no question that Don Inodoro, with all his defects as a mythic hero of the old school, is portrayed by Fontanarrosa as a bulwark against a whole spectrum of Argentine sociocultural pretensions that must be belied and discredited through the effective strategy of a merciless satire. The figure of Inodoro Pereyra is cut from an entirely popular piece of cloth, as is the sort of heavy-handed ironic language he uses (whether "deliberately" or as the result of the narrative stance his creator wishes to project). This quality enhances the attractiveness of the drawings—whose elements in the form of an expressionistic distortion are of a true artistic originality—and explains the commercial success that Fontanarrosa's work has enjoyed.

But the artist's demythifying rhetoric, the definition of an uncompromising position conveyed even more forcefully in the *Boogie, el aceitoso* series, serves to place his works in the tradition of a popular culture where the appeal to the mass reader is not just a marketing technique but rather a creativity for widespread acceptance in the service of the best forms of sociocultural commentary. In this sense, *Aventuras* is underlain by a controlling presupposition: the possibility for the reader to accept as a point of departure the decline in national values and the ideological virtue of an artistic reflection on that decline. Fontanarrosa's reflection involves a verbal and graphic humorism based on certain significant misunderstandings and linguistic abuses—commonplaces, florid metaphors, true poetic fallacies, and so on—which are eloquent in the healthy attitude they imply toward the Argentine of dominant vested interests whose prejudicial ideology is the principal source of the decline seen through the figure of Inodoro Pereyra.

PECADOR Y GUITARRERO

PLATE 4.1

PLATE 4.1 *continued*

PLATE 4.2

PLATE 4.2 continued

PLATE 4.3

PLATE 4.3 *continued*

Mafalda: The Ironic Bemusement

Argentina is a fertile ground for the editorial cartoon that comments either obliquely or directly on national events and concerns. Indeed, perhaps only Mexico and Brazil can approach the creative activity of Argentine cartoonists in this regard. The contributions and the sheer humorous originality of Quino (the pseudonym of Joaquín Salvador Lavado, born in 1932) have served now for almost two decades as a Latin American standard, both in the unique drawing or strip and in the continuous narrative creation *Mafalda*. There are ten *Mafalda* books, or collections of strips, in the original Argentine edition, and they have sold extensively in the original Spanish in both the Argentine edition (1967–1974) and in the Mexican reprint (1977). The numerous translations into other languages are complemented by the commemorative Spanish sampling of the ten years of the strip, which carries an introduction by the Italian semiologist Eco (1974). It would be no exaggeration to say that the continental and international diffusion of *Mafalda* parallels that of the writings of Jorge Luis Borges and Julio Cortázar as paragons of Argentine cultural talent.

Unfortunately, like the works of Julio Cortázar, *Mafalda* was a victim of the intense, implacable sociocultural repression that dominated Argentina from the mid-1960s until late 1984, with only a brief respite in the early 1970s (Clinton 1978). Although not proscribed, *Mafalda* paid the price of critical, liberal-style questioning. Nationalist sectors that dominated the Left in the early 1970s felt that its overt and implied demythifying commentaries on national foibles and pretensions were too "cutesy" and timid, while conservative segments tended to see the strip's perspective on everyday middle-class Argentine life as "smart-aleck" and symptomatic of the carping attitude toward national values that weakened the country as much as did radical guerrilla activity (see, for example, Hernández 1975; Steinberg 1971; "Mafalda Hopes . . ." 1976; "Quino" [1972]; Moix 1973; Rivera 1976b; Cañizal 1975; Meson 1981; Koch 1981; Horn 1976).

The result was Quino's decision in 1973 to cease drawing *Mafalda* and his subsequent departure from Argentina; he now resides in Italy. The issue in Quino's decision to silence *Mafalda* and to cut himself off from the national source of inspiration was, therefore, not the material threat of censorship (i.e., *Mafalda* remains a remarkable commercial success for both artist and publisher), but rather the chilling effect on creativity of a society where repression is not only overt but also a constant and ominous rumbling of warning directed against even the most modest manifestations of social nonconformity. It is a war of nerves that has destroyed many aspects of cultural continuity in Argentina, and Quino is undoubtedly one of the country's most notable artists to have been affected.

Mafalda is a little girl, about eight or nine years old, who lives with her solidly middle-class family in an unspecified section of Buenos Aires. She is surrounded by neighbors, forms of life, cultural artifacts that are also solidly middle class. Her playmates—five or six recurring figures in the strips—represent various types and concerns of society, all indicative of a conjunction of contemporary phenomena to be seen in the Argentine capital. Mafalda's distinguishing characteristic, the feature that makes her the projection of Quino's critical understanding of that conjunction, is her acute sensitivity, which is not shared by either playmates (who often kid her about it) or her elders (parents, teachers, other adults on the block who are frequently astonished and perplexed by her comments). In fact, a significant aspect of the strip is that the other characters rarely understand fully the meaning of what Mafalda says. Lest the reader believe that *Mafalda* is self-righteous social criticism that takes itself too seriously, it must be stressed that Quino's work is characterized by an extremely fine sense of the ridiculous. By virtue of this fundamentally humorous perspective, *Mafalda* never engages in angry attack but rather only in ironic bemusement, a factor that enhances markedly its entertainment value and hence its broad appeal.

The cleverness of *Mafalda* is based on unquestionable "rhetorical" or "literary" strategems of judicious inverismilitude.   To be sure, there is a documentary patina about *Mafalda*: the remarkably accurate representation of metonymic details of Argentine bourgeois daily life, Quino's superb ear for that special combination of pretentious verbosity and gritty urban turns of speech that characterize the dominant Buenos Aires sociodialect as represented in a mainline of twentieth-century narrative and theater, and the zeroing in on patterns of behavior that reveal significant underlying social and ethic values.   Concomitantly, Quino is astute enough to couch these aspects in ironic terms that alleviate the painful shock of recognition they inevitably propose to induce.

Yet, *Mafalda* is singularly inverisimilar—rhetorically artificial, if you will—in its handling of a stereotypic range of sociological types, the description of which reads like headings from a social historian's treatise on Buenos Aires (e.g., Mafud 1973; Moffatt 1967).   The character of Mafalda is strategically foregrounded in the sense that her perceptiveness is exaggeratedly greater than that of not only the children around her, but of the limited (if loving and considerate) adults in her world.   Moreover, both her verbalizations and her interior monologs evince levels of irony that go beyond intellectual precocity and social maturity.   Indeed, Mafalda has often been criticized as being simply the mouthpiece of the nonchild Quino, though it is reasonable to counter that the object of the strip is not documentary child psychology but artful verbal and visual representation.   Such a representation may be "rhetorical," but only in the positive sense, in which all significant cultural artifacts are strategic foregroundings and effective distortions of a putatively neutral "reality" (a point we shall return to in Chapter 8).

The following discussions of individual strips begin by directing attention to immediately suggested meaning. Nevertheless, to the extent that Quino's works are pervaded by complex ironies (whose complexity is only compounded for the reader who is not a member of Mafalda's own Buenos Aires middle class), and to the extent that much of the strip's humor derives from playing off Mafalda's unique perceptions and the stereotypic behavior of both the adults and the other children of her environment, a discussion based on some rather loosely deployed organizational principles of text production is useful for the purpose of more precisely gauging the texture of

Quino's works (see Masotta 1968).

The first example concerns specifically Mafalda's acute self-awareness, which is not simply the recognition of the shortcomings of her society, but a self-identification that, as with the existentialists, is a fundamental article of faith of a Latin American "raised consciousness." The lack of such a self-awareness is correspondingly a personal and social shortcoming (see Plate 5.1). Mafalda's friend Susanita is reading in a newspaper about typical world crises. To Mafalda's consternation, Susanita's reaction is "typically" Argentine: First, her discarding the paper is a flight from what is believed to be an escapable reality, and, second, her words of relief reflect the self-delusion that somehow Argentina, by virtue of its location at the "end of the world," is free from the tensions and failures that beleaguer the rest of the world. Susanita's sentiments are an Argentine version of the "I'm all right, Jack" syndrome, undoubtedly the holdover of nineteenth-century idealist New World myths about the corrupt Old World. Susana or Susanita, the epitome of tragicomic bourgeois commonplaces, is Mafalda's natural foil. So diametrically opposed are their perceptions of the national reality and their respective styles for verbalizing those perceptions—Susana is all cliché-ridden bombast, Mafalda is studiously ironic—that the shock of self-recognition for many a reader must inevitably derive from Quino's mercilessly documentary representations of a spectrum of prevailing attitudes and expressive registers in Susana, and the unrelenting deflation to which Mafalda often subjects them. As a consequence, Mafalda is berated throughout the strips for concerning herself with world issues that somehow are thought to be of no concern to her compatriots.

In another strip (see Plate 5.2), Mafalda senses the contrast between her comfortable, untroubled middle-class existence and a surrounding reality to which dissenters in Argentine society have been only partially successful in calling attention (see, for example, Verbitsky 1957). In addition to the ingeniousness of juxtaposing television programs and the national reality, the strip (which graphically is the framing of a frame of reference, the frames of the strip encompassing the train-window–TV-screen picture of national reality) depends on the recognition of how bad national reality is if, by comparison with it, television is good (since Argentines with discerning taste pride themselves on recognizing how bad national television is, with its dubbed versions of U.S. programs and its poor local imitations; see Muraro 1974).

Argentina, tied to the international market of more imposing capitalist countries, has, like many a smaller and less economically successful Third World society, had a difficult time maintaining its national mystique of identity. This is evident in changing life styles and the effect of foreign products on an extensive consumer society. Of course, *Mafalda* is unusually sensitive to this circumstance. It should be noted that Quino's perspective is not simply a boorish anti-Americanism; in one strip the humor is based on Mafalda's exclamation of relief when she discovers that, unlike numerous objects around her, her navel does not bear the inscription, "Made in Japan."

A preoccupation with the relationship between national or "autochthonous" values and foreign models in all areas of high and low culture is an abiding concern in Latin America. Argentina is no exception, and, indeed, it is arguable that some of the most vociferous debates on the subject have occurred in the press of that country. Unlike Mexico, Argentina has yet to define, if only on the level of sociopolitical and sociocultural myth, an all-embracing mystique of national identity. The result has been a justifiably proud Argentine tradition, but little broad-based consensus as to what, exactly, Argentine culture includes, or should include, beyond its intense brilliance and enormous vitality.

Nowhere is this issue more concentrated than in controversies concerning language. Argentine Spanish is sociolinguistically unique, and varieties of Buenos Aires Spanish bear unmistakable, aggressive stamps of identity. Buenos Aires Spanish manifests an array of foreign elements that run the gamut from fully assimilated items from the immigrant languages (basically Italian dialects and Yiddish) to the most recent imports from the language of TV (mostly English) and the newest commercial and technological products (English, French, and some Italian), with a traditional stock of English and French words and phrases relating to elite social rituals and phenomena (e.g., the worlds of afternoon tea, racing, country clubs, sports clothes, high fashion, and so on). Since all language belongs to clearly definable sociolinguistic contexts, it serves as a particularly prominent metonym for social values and patterns of cultural behavior. The pressure of foreign elements is tremendous, as it is on any urban setting, particularly when the language is not an internationally prestigious one.

The Spanish of Argentina has always been subject to "outside" influences, as is any language by the very nature of linguistic systems. This is the source of humor in the exchange concerning interjections uttered in the throes of violent, lawless death (Plate

5.3). The humor of this strip does not arise only from the interplay between "la pucha," which is not just Spanish but typically Argentine, and "aauugh," which only seems translinguistically onomatopoeic to a native speaker of English because it is a convention of his own language. It also derives from the clash between Felipe's naive anger (he is the ingenue, the "noble innocent," of the strip's cast of sociocultural stereotypes) and Mafalda's precocious figure of speech, "foreignizing deaths," which involves a hypallage or rhetorically misplaced modifier.

There are also several episodes that deal with ad language. Not only are advertisements seen, with the typical countercultural indignation of our age, as hypocritical, but their condescending exploitativeness is compounded by the use of foreign words; another aspect of this sociolinguistic issue is that such words are often incorrectly used, much as land developers in the U.S. Southwest rarely use correctly the Spanish words and phrases with which they attempt to glamorize their subdivisions and streets. The clash between Spanish and English is again highlighted by the foregrounded cleverness of Mafalda's rhetorical question (Plate 5.4). In yet another strip, Felipe meets Mafalda on the street and confesses that he has been unable to complete his homework, a theme on national independence. He says he decided to go for a walk in the hope of being inspired, but it did not work. Mafalda's only reply is to gaze goggle-eyed at the jungle of billboards touting foreign products in foreign languages that dwarf the streets. The implied rhetorical question is clear: In a foreign-dominated consumer society, "national independence" is a sham.

The core of Quino's strips, however, does not concern particularized barbs directed against social inequities, commercial and sociolinguistic foreign exploitation, or national loss of identity. Indeed, were the *Mafalda* strips based on heavy-handed social criticism, they would have as specialized a range of audiences as does, say, *Doonesbury*. In fact, *Mafalda's* enormous popularity in Argentina, Latin America, and internationally derives not from self-righteous exposés of the enormous problems that beset Argentina as one reasonable microcosm of Latin America, but from a typical, universal middle-class attitude that is especially prevalent in Argentina: We may be a screwed-up country, but it's the best, and all, we've got. This form of benevolent jingoistic exasperation with national foibles and weaknesses results in a blend of somewhat condescending irony (the artist and his audience are, because they see the problems, not afflicted by them) and Menippean satire (the shock of self-recognition induced by the artistic statement is therapeutically valid).

To the extent that the concern with national idiosyncrasies is central to Quino's strip, the issues dealt with constitute a broad spectrum of potentially humorous materials. Since the Argentines are seen as essentially idiosyncratic by most other Latin Americans, this emphasis on Quino's part has only contributed to, rather than hampered, his wide popularity. A random sampling of these issues reveals an emphasis on class consciousness, national self-images, patterns of social intercourse, social myths and hypocrisies, the relationship between cherished myths and perceived realities, socioeconomic aspirations, and aspects of family life that reveal the duplicity and hypocrisy of society at large. Because of its generally high standard of living for Latin America and an upper-class European influence, Argentina is notably "professionalized," and, as elsewhere in Latin America, the professions are held in exceptionally high esteem; so high, in fact, as to become a national shortcoming, as Plate 5.5 sardonically points out. The middle-class respectability of Mafalda's father's routine office job is overshadowed by the pompous superiority of the professional.

On the other hand, the next strip deals with more a tic of social intercourse than a serious sociopolitical defect (Plate 5.6). Any supposed national problem of buck-passing is reduced here to a tribal ritual to be learned by the uninitiated from the elders: Mafalda, who "suckles" as though at her mother's breast, versus the mother and the harried shoemaker. Sex roles under military tyranny have not been a particularly urgent topic of sociological and humanistic studies in Argentina. Although there have been many novels on the issue (see, e.g., Puig 1967, 1976; Medina 1976, 1977; Roffé 1976), the greater integration of women in the professions perhaps has made what is essentially an upper-middle- and middle-class preoccupation less a burning issue in Argentina than in the United States. Relative to standards of a raised consciousness, machismo and sexist male dominance are to be found in abundance in Argentina. There is no more dramatic Argentine cultural artifact to reflect this than the tango, both in the lyrics, in which the voice of the wronged Adam prevails, and in the dance, which is a ballet of male sexual assertion. Sex roles have yet to become, outside high cultural forms like novels that decry the *basurear*—the "trashing"—of women, a prominent issue of current social affairs. Nevertheless, several *Mafalda* strips suggest serious perspectives on the matter of sex roles. Once again, the fundamental exaggeration of Mafalda's foregrounded awareness and her ironic stance toward the sociocultural stereotypes of the children and adults of her world are the vehicles of commentary. In one strip (Plate 5.7), it is obvious that Susanita has assimilated uncritically a wide variety of commonplaces that are self-contradictory in the sense that they represent irreconcilable social goals for women. At issue is Susanita's opportunistic feminism (the full implications of which we can assume she does not grasp) and the bourgeois values that underlie it, versus Mafalda's distinction between legitimate women's rights and much sought-after class and social advantages that are used to identify a woman's relative position in a consumer-oriented society.

But in the final analysis, one of Quino's most ingenious contributions lies in the meticulous identification of the extensive array of small-beer social myths by which a complex urban society such as Buenos Aires defines and copes with its daily existence. In one of the few strips in which Mafalda's rhetorically heightened irony and perceptiveness are not the vehicles of commentary, her father has a shock of recognition as to both the falseness of the images of life created by exploitative advertising and the threatening world that it undertakes to conceal from us in directing our attention toward unattainable commercial ideals (Plate 5.8). Just as European immigrants dreamed of getting ahead in Argentina (the magic phrase was *hacer América*, "to make it in America"), many Argentines have dreamed of making it in the United States. Manolo, the son of Spanish immigrants who dreams of using his father's humble corner grocery store as the base for a new Rockefeller empire, brags about his brother's easy conquest of the United States (Plate 5.9).

Finally (Plate 5.10), Mafalda and Felipe engage in a typical Argentine social discourse: the problem of making ends meet. What is ironic is that these are no "hard times" down-and-outers worrying about a roof over their heads, or the impoverished widow washerwoman frantic about her inability to buy medicines for her sickly child. They are children of solid, comfortable bureaucrats and office workers who own an apartment, a car, a TV, and who go to the movies every week and the beach every summer. Yet they sound like desperate victims of a deep economic depression. Of course, they are, and the Argentine economic situation was seen by many as a grim national joke in the 1960s and the 1970s. The humor arises, of course, not only from the children's parroting of their parents' daily litany of complaints, but from the contradictions of a society no longer able to maintain with ease a very enviable standard of living.

In a certain sense, Mafalda's exasperation with Felipe's "survey of the middle class" must have echoed the feelings of many Argentines who recognized themselves and their concerns and pretensions in all too many of Quino's strips. That is one reason why *Mafalda* is at present a cultural artifact of a past, more relaxed Argentine society than the one prevailing today: Urbane humor is risky in a country still recovering from almost two straight decades of violence and chaos with little prospect of maintaining an open society in the foreseeable future. Quino's work is now devoted almost exclusively to highly intellectual and more subtle one-time strips that, despite their critical acclaim, stand little chance of the mass audience *Mafalda* enjoyed. But if *Mafalda* is for the time being history, it is a body of cultural texts well worth preserving. As Mafalda herself said when she tossed aside the children's book *El maravilloso mundo que nos rodea* to go play outside in the real world: "Pero ¡sea! Vamos a enfrascarnos con la realidad."

PLATE 5.1

PLATE 5.2

PLATE 5.3

PLATE 5.4

PLATE 5.5

PLATE 5.6

PLATE 5.7

PLATE 5.8

PLATE 5.9

PLATE 5.10

6

Sol de Noche and the
Graphic Humor of *Superhumor*

The illustrated magazine *Superhumor* is a subsidiary or parallel publication of *Humor registrado*, which the Ediciones de la Urraca began publishing in 1978. I have been unable to determine the exact year in which *Superhumor* began to appear, but I would guess its inaugural number appeared some time in 1979. What I do know as a matter of fact is that *Humor registrado*—in reality, the parent (and most lucrative) publication of a cluster of materials published by the people associated with Ediciones de la Urraca—was banned briefly by the Argentine government in late 1982. Those who practice professionally the analysis of Latin American culture would, in our reprehensible but not altogether misguided skepticism, prefer to believe that it is precisely the unrelenting scrutiny of national issues, the uncompromising burlesquing and satirizing of pretensions, commonplaces, and outright, disingenuous duplicity of the government that make such publications as *Humor registrado* and *Superhumor* powerful contenders for attention in the national dialog. After all, Argentines, like most people, are probably more influenced and swayed by a pithy editorial cartoon than by a weighty, albeit more cogently reasoned, newspaper editorial or sociopolitical essay. Humor magazines sell very well in Argentina, despite their high cover price, and Ediciones de la Urraca won a very substantial market in the decade of its operations beginning during a very inauspicious moment for publishing in Argentina.

It is worth recalling at this point that Argentina is the leading country in Latin America in the production of graphic publications and in the development of an extensive inventory of graphic narrative and graphic humor titles that place it in the forefront of cartoon art in the Third World.   Mexico has a flourishing comic book trade, but with the exception of names like Rius, there are very few truly outstanding artists to compete with the Argentines, whose accumulated experience dates back to the late 1920s, one of the most halcyon periods of Argentine culture in general.

Thus, a publication like *Superhumor* (which, if *Humor registrado* belongs to the genre of *Mad Magazine*, is an intellectual or sophisticated version of mass humor magazines) drew from a large pool of established and well-trained artists and writers for the preparation of its material, and many of the names it featured have well-deserved international reputations among cartoon art connoisseurs. The contents of the *Superhumor* issues range over a broad spectrum of materials and styles, from narrative strips that deal with specifically national themes in various registers of allegorization and metaphorization, through strips that offer very imaginative interpretations of universal issues such as individual identity or social foibles, to strips that provide a specifically Argentine interpretation of the Third World and international questions such as human violence or U.S. imperialism. In addition, *Superhumor* published literary contributions as well as material providing analytical commentary on popular culture topics, such as the tenth-anniversary study of Quino's *Mafalda* and interviews with and historical material on major Argentine graphic artists. For this reason, *Superhumor* was a sort of "metacomic book," a publication that provided as much the opportunity for reflection on the nature and place of cartoon art in Argentine and Latin American popular culture as it provided actual graphic humor materials as did any other of the many cartoon periodicals and comic books in Argentine art history.

I would like to focus my discussion of the materials of *Superhumor* and the strategies for creating meaning and sociocultural commentary through graphic art in the strip *Sol de Noche*. *Sol de Noche* is written by Guillermo Saccamanno, a *guionista* of impressive credentials and a long record of work in the field. The strip is drawn by Patricia Breccia, about whom I have little concrete information, though I know that she is the daughter of

Alberto Breccia, one of the truly great Argentine cartoon artists. (I might note that it is customary, in "high" Argentine cartoon work, for a strip to be the collaborative effort of a writer and an artist, both often with their own independent reputations. There are, of course, notable exceptions, like the *Mafalda* materials of Quino and *Las aventuras de Inodoro Pereyra* and *Boogie, el aceitoso* series of Roberto Fontanarrosa.)

The following are principal features of *Sol de Noche:*

1. The main characters of the strip are the Garfieldesque cat Barbieri, and a hip but equally reflective young woman.

2. Barbieri is identified by his formal attire, down to a bow tie that he wears on all occasions, and by his highly stylized, angular outline. By contrast, Sol de Noche is identified by her exaggerated mass of hair, which floats around her like a cloud, and by her loose and transparent clothes that accentuate the details of her woman's body.

3. Sol de Noche moves, in a somewhat "spacey" fashion, through the streets and living spaces of Buenos Aires, commenting in both a bemused and a resigned way on aspects of the hypocrisy, alienation, and insensitivity of people as integers of a mass society. In this sense, Sol de Noche is a transformation of the *poète maudit,* a privileged but suffering observer of the human condition. In the tradition of much popular Argentine literature, Sol de Noche exemplifies, rather stereotypically, the perceptive but slightly neurotic Argentine woman whose life style is the attempt to be a free spirit in a society that is noted for its Victorian restrictions on self-expression and its repression of the sensuous or the sexual (indeed, the recurring themes of the material in *Superhumor* concentrate insistently on varieties of Marcusian Eros versus Civilization, with the latter personified in the country's long and dreary tradition of brutal military regimes).

4. Sol de Noche's name is metaphor for her stance toward her society. In the first place, the expression as a lexical item is the trade name for a type of outdoor lantern, which has become a common noun in Argentine Spanish. Thus, Sol de Noche is, to use an English-language clichéd metaphor, a "ray of sunshine" in the spiritual and emotional night of her surrounding society. Significantly, we usually see Sol de Noche moving through Argentine society at night, on dates, at parties, attending cultural events in the context of Buenos

Aires's very active and variegated night life. These contexts
are treated in the strip as synecdoches of the qualities of
Argentine society as a whole, and Sol de Noche's interaction
with them, her interior monologs about them, her comments
to her cat Barbieri, and his interior monologs about her
reactions in turn are all fragmentary, overlapping texts that
specify a particular form of discourse on unassuming but
significant aspects of Argentine social life.

For example, one strip (February 1982) concerns the
pseudosophistication of Buenos Aires's version of the beautiful
people. "Cuando huye el diá," like many but not all of the strips,
focuses specifically on Buenos Aires night life as a metonymy of
primary cultural values: Night life in Buenos Aires is both
considerable and a barometer of events in the country, to the extent
that certain phenomena and spectacles reflect explicitly as well as
obliquely the prevailing parameters of behavior allowed by the
dictatorship in power. Of course, Sol de Noche's name is ironically
metaphoric, in the sense that her feelings and comments "illuminate"
the nighttime scene.   In "Cuando huye el día," there is a clear
juxtaposition between Sol de Noche leading an uneventful,
"wholesome" day under the sun and retiring early with a good book
(Kafka), only to be interrupted in the last stage of the routine by a
call to join a hip party in progress.

The strip provides a number of interesting markers of the
disjunction between Sol de Noche's daytime activities and the after-
hours party she is asked to join. Although the lines of the strip are,
in general terms, quite garishly expressionistic, there is no question
as to the attractive simplicity of the scenes in which Sol de Noche
pursues the wholesome pleasures of watering her plants,
sunbathing, strolling through the plaza, and relaxing with a good
book. Linguistically, these activities are marked by easy vocabulary
and direct sentences, of identical grammatical structure, which
sound as if they were taken from a first-year language text: "Me lavo
los dientes," "Entro a un cine," "Me acuesto temprano." By contrast,
the party scene abounds in grotesque images, both the physical
aspect of the hostess and her guests and the nature of the clothes
they wear and the attitudes they strike. Most striking is the
language in which they speak. It is a parody of the sort of ludicrous
and pseudoinventive jargon one associates with social pretensions
and an "in-crowd." In place of the verbally laconic and graphically
balanced panels corresponding to Sol de Noche's daytime space, the
party scene is congested, with overlapping figures, actions, and

speeches that would seem to serve to signify a cacophonous din: If Sol de Noche feels like a *cucaracha* snuggled up in bed reading Kafka, she enters the teeming, roach-like setting of her friend's party.

The linguistic markers of the party are the extravagant blend of faddish slang and current stylish topics of conversation, and the sort of indiscriminate use of purportedly sophisticated words and phrases to be found among the socially pretentious. For example, the hostess's invitation includes the two phrases "[La fiesta] tiene una onda brutal" and "Mató mil flaca." When Sol de Noche arrives (Plate 6.1), she is assaulted by the following linguistic mishmash: "Pasá, Sol. Están todos. No falta nadie. El tout Baires. Gente de lo más. Date una idea. Un vernisage contuti. Pasá la bien y hacé la tuya. Esta noche viene super!!! Están los poetas, los plásticos, los analistas, los arquitectos y todas las modelos . . . Con decirte que hasta Manliba mandó una delegación." It is not that people in Buenos Aires do not talk this way: They do, and the speech is an accurate parody of the sort of blend of foreign phrases and trendy Spanish that characterize a particular form of cultural discourse. The guests speak about the need for a "cambio de estructuras," "concentración Zen," and "la era de Acuario." One guest insists, "No me confundas, yo soy gay de puro macho, che," and a chorus line of guests proclaim the prized activities of the day: "¡Yo estuve en Danza Abierta! ¡Yo en las Jornadas! ¡Yo en Teatro Abierto! ¡Yo en el Encuentro de las Artes! ¡Y yo soy semióloga del arte impreso!"

This sort of language provides vacuous expression in place of the previous description of Sol de Noche's simple pleasures, and garish linguistic structures replace the simple declarative sentences that Sol de Noche uses to refer to her routine. Taken aback by this context, her response is to articulate a new series of simple declarative sentences that describe her hasty retreat from the party: "Apagué el pucho no. 100," "Trastabillé contra el vaso no. 50," "Y pisé uno de los plomos no. 1." Free from the oppressive setting of the party, Sol de Noche returns home via a number of stages described in predominantly unforegrounded language. Sol de Noche returns home, hoping to find refuge in the company of her cat, only to find that he has gone off to "noviar en el tejado de zinc caliente." She laments the fact that: "Todos los hombres son iguales y si son gatos, peor."

In "Ol Dat Tangou" (July 1981), Sol de Noche is the narrator of the story of Goyo, the broken-down tango singer. Where in the first strip we have examined she is the central protagonist of a situation and the legends of the strips provide a third-person commentary on her interaction with that situation, in this case Sol de Noche's interaction becomes that of a commentary to the reader on Goyo's sorry plight. What is particularly humorous about this commentary is that Sol de Noche's role is not strictly interpretive in the sense of explaining to us the meaning of the scenes we see depicted; she does not, in other words, fulfil the classic role of the third-person narrator who mediates between the reader and a situation by interpreting it from the perspective of privileged knowledge.

Rather, Sol de Noche's commentary is literally a translation of the dialogs of Goyo's world. The clever silliness of this situation is compounded by the fact that Goyo speaks in Lunfardo, the argot of the world of the Italian immigrants and the tango, a sociolect that has become the quintessence of Buenos Aires Spanish, particularly within any context of popular culture. In the strip, Goyo and his aged girl friend (his *percanta*) speak Lunfardo, and Sol de Noche reexpresses them in "standard" Spanish. Barbieri, Sol de Noche's cat, who performs with Goyo, speaks Gatuno, which Sol de Noche translates for the reader; when Barbieri utters something that seems like Spanish, Sol de Noche reexpresses that in Gatuno. If the heroine's principal function is to interpret, her speeches are marked by the tag, "Que traducido quiere decir que . . ." In one panel, they arrive at the door of a club called La Giralda, and Sol de Noche remarks: "Que traducido quiere decir que asi llegamos a La Giralda."

The action of the strip revolves around Sol de Noche's brilliant idea for Goyo and Barbieri to become rock singers, a change that is even more disastrous in fortunes than their luck as tango stars. When the young audience drives them off the stage with imprecations of anger, Sol de Noche's translation is: "Que traducido quiere decir guarda que nos rompen el espiritu." In general terms, then, the sense of "Ol Dat Tangou" has to do with the versions of popular music culture in Buenos Aires. Sol de Noche's responsibility as an interpreter of the language of these versions is a drolly ironic commentary on the conventions they involve, with the significant conjunction of tango argot, rock slang, and Barbieri's "caterwauling" as only different aspects of the same phenomenon. Actually, the strip is a vindication of the tango culture, because, having been repudiated by the folk music audience, the characters make a closing declaration of support for the modern greats of the tango in Argentina. Significantly, Sol de Noche does not interpret this declaration.

Breccia's drafting is particularly interesting for the creative manner in which Argentine society is evoked. There is a strong current of expressionistic graphic art in Argentine cartooning, and Breccia is only one of a number of contributors to *Superhumor* for whom the only way to render the complex, oppressive, garish, and degrading nature of their society is through an aggressively anti-cute and anaesthetic art. Equally, there are a number of cartoonists who use language in similarly symptomatic ways (Fontanarrosa is the one who has clearly established an international reputation in this regard). All forms of artistic discourse are metaphoric on various levels, and the metaphoric cleverness of Breccia and others lies in the specific troping in which they engage, based on the various forms of linguistic and graphic clichés identified with a specific Latin American cultural frame of reference.

PLATE 6.1

PLATE 6.1 *continued*

7

Overcoming National Reality:
Las puertitas del Sr. López
of Trillo and Altuna

Las puertitas del Sr. López, according to its subtitle, is a collection of "25 complete comic strips," with text by Carlos Trillo and drawings by Horacio Altuna. The strip appeared originally in the magazine *El Pérdulo* from September to December 1979; from March 1980 to October 1981, it appeared in *Humor registrado,* presently Argentina's leading humor magazine.

According to Trillo (private communication), the strip was abandoned because it was felt that the topic dealt with had run its course. This is a praiseworthy decision when one contemplates the repetition to which even the most creative strips inevitably succumb. At the same time, *Las puertitas* is only one of the successful series produced by the Trillo-Altuna team, which counts among its accomplishments *Los reportajes del Loco Chávez,* on the tics and manias of the Argentine middle class as scrutinized by Loco Chávez, and *Merdechesky,* a strip that appears in the magazine *Superhumor. Merdechesky* follows the misadventures of a naive detective of Jewish-Polish extraction in the jungle of New York. In a certain sense this strip echoes the interpretation of North American violence portrayed by Fontanarrosa in his highly successful *Boogie, el aceitoso.*

The publication of the strips of *Las puertitas* in book form, with an introduction by Juan Sasturain, stands as a sort of memorial to the success of the series and confirms its importance as representative of the *Humor registrado* and *Superhumor* genre within the large arena of contemporary Argentine graphic humor.

The interest of this chapter lies in examining the sociocultural contexts of *Las puertitas* and with studying the artistic strategies employed to create a specific critical position vis-à-vis Argentine society. It is obvious that *Las puertitas* exemplifies a type of popular culture product that, on the one hand, manifests strategies that appeal to the mass distribution of graphic material: That is to say, it identifies with the mass circulation of humor magazines. On the other hand, the strip makes use of certain cultural patterns for the purpose of making a biting and penetrating commentary on a range of social aspects of society, aspects considered degrading and thus available for an analytical presentation with the goal of arousing in the reading public a conscious reaction to those aspects.

Recent analyses of Latin American popular culture have shown that there exists very clearly a type of artistic creation that relies for its mass distribution on its utilization of the patterns of mass culture. At the same time, these patterns are meant to be pressed into the service of a fundamentally creative and critical enterprise such that the contribution of these procedures is to effect some sort of sociocultural interpretation. In this sense, such popular phenomena as *Las puertitas del Sr. López* are essentially no different from the most prestigious Latin American fiction. If in the novels of writers such as the Mexican Jorge Ibargüengoitia, the Argentine Manuel Puig, and the Peruvian Mario Vargas Llosa, we find an artistic mode that seeks to identify itself with so-called high culture, these graphic works also reveal the use of mass culture patterns to achieve an identification between the novel and a range of Latin American sociocultural problems that may be productively examined from the perspective of those patterns.

As a consequence, the flotsam and jetsam of mass culture in Puig, or the examples of soap operas and other popular narratives in Vargas Llosa are strategies for underscoring the contact between an artistic form that is identified with the cultural interests of a limited audience (i.e., the readers of high-culture novels) and a group of concerns that impinge on Latin American society as a whole. By contrast, what we have in the case of works like *Las puertitas* is the attempt to expropriate popular culture as such, as a point of contact for a generalized problem. Owing to the depth of analysis made possible through popular culture modes, at issue also is the demonstration of how mass phenomena can achieve a level of analysis as challengingly penetrating as that for which more elitist works typically strive.

In this sense, an adequate treatment of the Trillo-Altuna strip would have to study not only what the technical and graphic achievements are, but also how the latter contribute to the realization of the proposed goal of treating a sociocultural problem. It is undeniable that the artistic quality of the drawings is outstanding (within the genre of graphic realism) and that it is indicative of the best of such work in Argentina in terms of the handling of planes, frame composition, subtlety of images, and the narrative flow that links individual frames. One must note in particular in this regard the utilization of essentially "photographic" aspects toward the sense of an accurate rendering of the texture of life in urban Buenos Aires.

These naturalistic aspects alternate on the one hand with the grotesqueness of certain features that are highlighted (the self-satisfied nature of López's wife, the barely contained enviousness and violence of his fellow workers) and, on the other hand, the ruptures and fanciful parentheses that make up the contrapuntal world beyond, which López makes out behind the "little doors" in the rooms in which he moves.

Our concern here, then, is not to explore the graphic merits of the strips, but rather to study which are the rhetorical mechanisms they reveal toward achieving a level of sociocultural commentary. Like many mass culture phenomena that show the sort of highly creative impulse of interest to us here, *Las puertitas* reveals, as its primordial feature, an interpenetration of, a fluctuation between what is characteristically documentary in the images and the aforementioned expressionistic openings. That is to say, these strips fulfil a criterion of documentary fidelity as regards the representation of the texture of middle-class life in Buenos Aires, and they achieve a notable level of "photographism" in their depiction of crucial details of this prototypic life style.

In marked contrast to this aspect, we have the transition toward what, for lack of a better term, we can call an expressionistic criterion. This transition serves as the point of departure for exploring another sense, a substratum of meaning beyond the apparently complete and self-sufficient texture of things. The strict materiality of daily life conceals the "beyond of meaning" that the strategy of juxtaposition on which the strip is based is concerned with unmasking. Thus, on one level, López and his environment synthesize an image that we could almost call exaggeratedly documentary of a middle-class Buenos Aires office worker. We see López moving among his urban settings, his home (where his wife is the quintessence of bourgeois materialism, with her modest social, economic, and class pretensions) and his office, where the degrading nature of desk-bound tasks so ably described by writers like the Argentines Roberto Arlt and Roberto Mariani, the Uruguayan Mario Benedetti, and a long literary tradition is evoked: López plays the part of the victim of a humiliating structural oppression set in motion by the mechanisms of the office. By the same token, these mechanisms are personified by his egotistical and parvenu colleagues and by the bossism of the office supervisor. Special emphasis is given to the fierce competition and thoughtless cruelty that holds sway in the interpersonal relation of the setting in which our protagonist and antihero moves.

To the foregoing is also added the lack of organization that in turn provokes disorientation in the individual because he does not know which responsibility to fulfil. In this way, the office, becomes the microcosm of an oppressive and degrading society. As counterweights to his home and the office, where his spirit is eroded by stultifying work routines, there are the spaces of the great metropolis that function as paradigms of the life styles of modern man: the individual at work; taking the bus; making his way through streets crowded with faceless people. At every turn, we see López as a sort of pilgrim, moving among the different living spaces of his physical and spiritual worlds, spaces that underscore over and over again a materialistic world that is emotionally devalued and humiliating.

In this sense, López is a character who serves to attract a series of key phenomena in a repressive society. He feels—and sees—himself constantly under attack by an unthinking and heartless society that humiliates him with degrading offenses. One ought to stress that, if López is a hypersensitive target that registers vividly every event of man's belittlement, he deals with a society that is markedly insensitive toward the individual. That is to say, for the purposes of the strip, it is important to emphasize how López's fellow men are unable to realize how brutish and mean-minded they are. For example, Sra. López is a distinctly unattractive—even repugnant—woman, and we are shown the long-suffering and silent, but nonetheless eloquent, reactions of her husband to her posturings, his shudderings of distaste in the face of this puffy and painted mound of flesh whose feigned elegance is nothing more than gross and vulgar.

If López is a "pilgrim" who moves from one living space to another in this degrading and humiliating world, our antihero's world is fractured by a series of critical moments in terms of the controlling image of the door that opens to permit the crossing of the threshold separating the oppressive here from a fantasmagoric suprareality of there. The reality to which López is permitted access is a suprareality in the sense that, in Freudian or psychoanalytic terms, it constitutes a space wherein he is able to resolve, albeit only momentarily, the conflicts that befall him as the result of the disjunction between his nature as a timid, sensitive, and repressed individual and the crass thoughtlessness of the world about him.

All of the strips contain three structural "movements." There is the establishment of a specific daily context, followed by a crisis. As a consequence, López seeks refuge behind a bathroom door (the bathroom being one of the only private sanctuaries left to modern man); this incursion into the beyond, thanks to the access provided by the door, permits a reenactment of the crisis encountered in the world of day-to-day living. Once this crisis has been resolved or purged thanks to its reenactment, whether by a more felicitous denouement or through the greater ability to comprehend its nature as the result of a fanciful representation of it, López retreats from the secret refuge to return to everyday reality. At times, López makes the transition back to everyday reality of his own accord, though on occasion he is "restored" to reality involuntarily as though awakening from a nightmare or from an erotic dream.

In one strip we see how the emphasis of the narrative line lies typically with a question of strictly everyday, interpersonal relations (Plate 7.1). There is a prevalence of the image over words, underscoring thereby López's basic "aphony" and his contemplation, from behind his eyeglasses, of the circumstance in which he finds himself floundering—the imperative to confront a test, which in this case involves the far from seductive sexual demands of his wife. López seeks refuge through a door into a suprareality—in this case, an erotic daydream—that allows him to return to the real world and fulfil honorably the obligations imposed upon him. Although this example makes use of the shopworn erotic fantasy as a stimulus for the sexual act, what bears emphasizing here is that the demands of the woman, signalled by the grotesque details of her kittenish behavior and her provocative négligée, are turned into yet one more trap/test for López in the arduous pilgrimage of his daily existence.

López, as a consequence, is no hero: His very name is as

common and ordinary as is possible. He is a poor unfortunate tormented by the mean-minded people around him and by the values and structures of behavior with which, by implied consent, they burden him. He is a type that in the final analysis is unable to deal with his society; thus his escape and his refuge behind the doors, like a scared child who must hide from what cannot be physically or emotionally faced, turn out to be a form of copping out of a reality that is for him too harsh and oppressive. The foregoing could lead one to conclude that, by contrast with cultural artifacts where an immediate reality and a surrealistic or suprarealistic fantasy are juxtaposed, and the movement toward fantasy becomes a productive mechanism for resolving the immediate oppressive experiences, in the case of the López strips such a movement is only a respite for rest and reflection. In no way can it be said that the movement from reality to fantasy allows López to resolve more than momentarily his conflicts or arms him, like a Marvel comics hero, to right wrongs. Rather, it is more an effective way for him to take stock of those conflicts in order better to face them as part of the undeniable texture of a degraded human existence.

López is ultimately unable to take on the oppressive patterns in order to modify them. Instead, he achieves a level of profound pathos in his fundamental inability to alter the world to which he must irremediably return. From the point of view of the sort of communication with the readers sought by the strips, one can say that the former are asked to identify themselves, no matter how ruefully, with López as part of an opportunity to understand a commonly shared plight. If there is a central concern in *Las puertitas* that validates the psychoanalytical aspects used, it is the dominant pattern of censorship, and the repression the latter engages in. Fantasy of the sort López takes refuge in thereby becomes, in psychoanalytic terms, a compensation for a truth censored in our everyday world. This is the case in the episode shown in Plate 7.2.

The jackboot mentality of the severe *paterfamilias* toward the legitimate interests of his son, the imperious order for him to shut up ("a mí no me discute nadie"), and the threats of psychological and physical punishment that he wields to impose his will, with the support and acquiescence of his wife, are duplicated in the sequence of images in the world López discovers beyond the door: The Gestapo-like appearance of the agents of order, the thoroughly repressed and subjugated populace, the swift and sure attack on the individual who shows any sign of rebellion, and, above all else, the eloquence of the wordless balloons that attest to the expressive sanitation that has been achieved.

There is, nevertheless, one aspect of this pattern that remains unresolved. If the door closes in the end, it would seem to insinuate that the alternative vision achieved by López remains beyond our reach, if not as what is forbidden, at least as what is fundamentally unattainable. If one of the goals of the artistic materials we have identified as truly original in its innovating artistic criterion is to stimulate a productive critical stance in the reader toward the structures of his degraded and repressive society, the representation of this condition to which *Las puertitas* aspires could be considered basically cut off by the image of the door to the beyond of explicit and direct understanding, which slams shut.

It is undeniable that the protagonist's anguish synthesizes his fundamental concern: López is unable to speak the truth of his relation with his fellow workers or the conflicts that he experiences in his endless dealings with the functionaries he comes into contact with in the business of daily life in a city like Buenos Aires. Nor can he express himself concerning the generalized diminishment of the human being, or, more specifically, the humiliating way in which he is treated by his domineering wife, who is a veritable Argentine version of James Thurber's devouring domestic females.

What is involved here as López's productive participation in his setting is the voyeur spied upon. The reader is obliged to fulfil the role of a voyeur contemplating López as a voyeur of his own society, the individual who appropriates the right to spy, without blinking, on the sordid human condition manifest in the daily conduct of one's neighbor. The reader in turn becomes assimilated to López's vision as he witnesses him witnessing and is endowed thereby with the same scrutinizing privilege and with the same ability to comprehend the signs of the thoughtless human behavior that the strip focuses on.

In some of the strips there is a gesture toward defiance and rebellion on López's part. But in general he is resigned. In the eyes of his fellow men, he is reasonably seen as one more stunted and tame individual, subjugated by his circumstance. But it is his inner world, the world he creates in the face of his daily existence, that is all that allows him—and us, as a consequence of the creative artifact—to return to reality and to continue to function within it. There can be little doubt that López is a pathetic and, in a certain sense, a dishonest person as a consequence of his evasion in favor of a suprareality that removes him from what he is unable to face directly.

But López is essentially an individual who has been rendered dishonest by a dishonest and profoundly hypocritical society. As a consequence, the productive interplay of the Trillo-Altuna strip between the two worlds of his consciousness is legitimated. In this way, artistic creation—López's fantasy, Trillo-Altuna's strip—becomes a gesture of honesty in the face of a harsh reality that, to the extent that it cannot be argued away, must be dealt with in some way that will keep the individual from being drowned by it.

PLATE 7.1

PLATE 7.2

PLATE 7.2 *continued*

continued *overleaf*

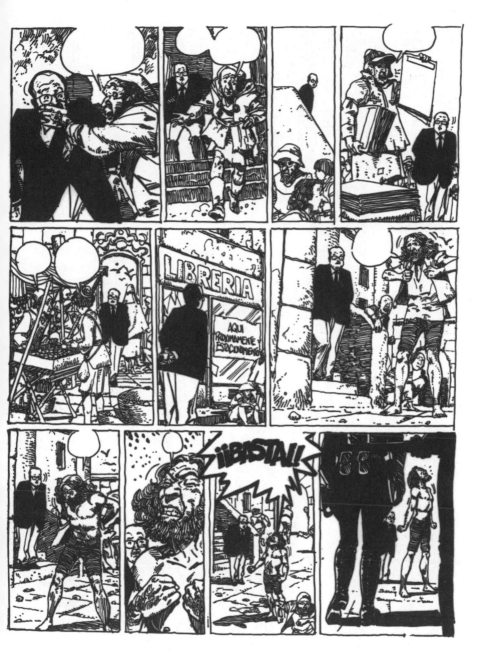

continued overleaf

8

Los Supermachos:
Golpe de estado en San Garabato

 A perennial problem in the study of graphic arts material is that of choosing which example or issue of a series to examine in detail. That is to say, there is so much material, so many titles in a series like *Los Supermachos*, that it becomes impossible to study all the issues to the same degree, just as there is something rather arbitrary about limiting the discussion to a few examples. I have chosen *Golpe de estado en San Garabato* (No. 575 in the series; of which a few pages are reproduced here) a little by chance. But I am convinced that it demonstrates superbly how the team of writers and artists who continue the creation of Rius (Eduardo del Río) focuses on sociopolitical and cultural themes throughout the large number of issues published in the series. To be sure, there is an advantage in the study of long-running series, such as *Los Supermachos, Los agachados, Kalimán,* or *El Payo*, that does not apply in the case of so-called "high" culture, and that is the high incidence of uniformity from one text to the next in a series. That is to say, it is possible to make almost the same observations about all of the issues of a particular comic; the same comments on content, language, drawing style. In short, there is a high degree of homogeneity about any one issue that it shares easily and obviously with other issues, such that taken together the issues really make up one artistic whole.

This circumstance differs from that of high culture works, where the relative autonomy from one work to another of any author is prized, and where works usually are not fragmented into an endless series of repetitive examples such as is the case with a popular and successful creation like *Los Supermachos*. Therefore, it should not be surprising to find in popular culture products a criterion more of uniformity than variety or originality from one number to the next. And in large measure the success of the product depends on this uniformity and the absence of any great surprises or significant ruptures as concerns the creative purpose.

Thus, that this issue of *Los Supermachos* has been chosen a little arbitrarily should not detract from its representativeness as far as the nature of the series is concerned as a unified work of popular art. The plot of *Golpe* may be summarized in the following terms: After a series of frames in which Calzonzín (the main character of the series) complains about how things never change, he runs into Doña Emerencia (the town *beata*), who tells him about a prize to be awarded to whoever can demonstrate the physical existence of the human soul. Almost all of the inhabitants charge off after the prize, and those who are left behind—the stock characters of the strip—decide to effect a coup d'état and do away with the oppressive regime of Don Perpetuo del Rosal. But as we see that the coup only serves to shuffle the opportunities for one group to exploit another, Don Perpetuo returns and reasserts his power despite the stubbornness of Don Lucas, the pseudorevolutionary who thirsts for the chance to indulge in abuses of power. The text closes with Don Lucas fleeing out into the countryside, where he maintains that he is the town president in exile.

One of the constants in *Los Supermachos* is the artistic image that fluctuates between the markedly costumbristic or local-color and the markedly expressionistic or antirealistic. By markedly costumbristic, I mean an image whose details have some sort of documentary value as regards the characters, their settings, and natural, historic, and social situations as projected by the strip. For example, we can identify a series of thoroughly local-color features, like the use of a certain kind of clothing, details about professions and occupations and the social class of the characters (the pharmacist's tie and vest, the *beata's* black and formless garb, etc.), as well as the gestures and the "typical" behavior patterns of a gallery of stereotypically identifiable Mexicans. All of these elements function to present a specifically rural Mexican setting, the Mexico typified by the fictitious village of San Garabato.

At the same time, these details that identify the common denominator of the strip serve also to underscore the pretentious antics that make up the weak suit of the town the comic focuses on. In this way, *Los Supermachos* identifies squarely with one of the dominant features of popular culture: the element of caricature projected by the characters and by the unambiguous contexts in the process of referring to a familiar social scene. This is why these figures have no pretense at profundity or semantic density as human types. It is enough for them to be transparent indexes of a national local color.

On the other hand, the element of caricature gives way to the expressionistic features. Like a counterweight to the strictly documentary image, these are details based on an obvious exaggeration or distortion of the costumbristic or realistic imperative. These images approach the ridiculous or the grotesque and deviate toward a noteworthy lack of verisimilitude as regards the details themselves and what they seem to signify. One need only consider the case of Calzonzín: To the caricature of the Mexican wrapped in his blanket is added the ludicrous note that it is an electric one. Calzonzín has added a cord and plug to his modest blanket, thereby giving it a grotesque "modernized" appearance. Thus, the caricature takes on expressionistic touches thanks to this distortion of what one would normally expect: It would be difficult to accept the possibility of such a detail in the case of a typical rural Mexican, and even less so in view of the fact that, aside from the bar and the "town hall," the town probably is not electrified. It is this sort of grotesque detail that is foregrounded to the detriment of the costumbristic image in *Los Supermachos*.

The grotesque touch extends to many of those who make up the world of San Garabato—for example, Lechuzo's oversized baseball cap; the exaggeratedly Spanish features of the bar's owner (his beret, his cigar, his hairy arms, along with the colloquial Spanish aspects of his speech). This ambivalence between costumbrism and expressionism also extends to language. On the one hand, the characters all speak a markedly Mexican Spanish (the bar owner excepted, of course). This linguistic Mexicanism often approaches the grotesque or the distorted when the characters begin to make plays on words or double entendres, or when conflicts arise between the Spanish of the bar owner and that of the other characters. As a consequence, we may find a Mexicanism appearing as a surprise element, with the Spaniard coming back with "one of his own" as an equally foregrounded element. His lines are filled with phrases like *Vamos, pues entonces, rediez, joder, ¡que va!, Usté,* and of course, a panoply of *vosotros* forms all in direct conflict with the often excessively Mexican touches of the speech of the Sangarabateños.

In sum, graphic elements as well as features of the speech of the characters waver between the "aggressively" costumbristic and colloquial, and what is markedly distorted and grotesque. It is the movement from insouciant caricature to the elaboration of exaggerated detail that I have called here the expressionistic counterweight in *Los Supermachos.*

As far as the handling of language is concerned in *Golpe de estado en San Garabato,* we can discern a basic series of processes and tensions. On the one hand, linguistic expression sustains the development of a story about some value, some happening, some element of Mexican social-cultural life. Thus, we read the conversations of the characters (and it is necessary to emphasize how one of the characteristics of *Los Supermachos* is the lack of transitions on the part of the narrator, by contrast with many comic books where parenthetical frames of written text serve to move from one segment to another of the story; *Los Supermachos* requires that we grasp transitions on the basis of the characters' speeches and the corresponding drawings). By virtue of these conversations we strive to understand what element of Mexican life is the issue dealt with in the comic under scrutiny. It is also to be supposed that we are concerned with determining what the position of the text is vis-à-vis this element and the features that illustrate it.

As a consequence, we count on the language being transparent or "referential" with respect to the meaning of the gross content of the work. The latter is surely the consequence, in terms of the legitimate expectations of the reader, of expression in popular culture and its relative and characteristic lack of ambiguity and signifying complexity in terms of the semantics of the cultural artifact. In this sense, the language of the comic book invites us to recognize the extent to which it deals in explicit meaning. Otherwise, we either could not read the text or reading it would be an interpretative task that would end up excluding an important spectrum of readers unaccustomed or indisposed to reading a text that problematizes language rather than views it is a vehicle of concrete meaning.

Yet, at the same time and also as a counterweight to the facilely costumbristic or documentary, we encounter in the text word plays and puns that border on the meaningless, on the absence of transparent meaning. It is therefore evident that there are expressions in *Los Supermachos* where the linguistic jokes, the double entendres, and simply the distortion of language by the characters come close to a lack of meaning. An example of this comes when Calzonzín says: "¡Compañeros! ¡Vivir fuera del presupuesto, es vivir en la vil inopia!" These words, which are a parody of a typical campaign cliché, serve as an unintentionally failed attempt to imitate the rhetoric and the slogans of politicians. The result of this effort at imitation is something that reminds us of a campaign slogan precisely because its meaning is tenuous, being little more than a series of words bearing some resemblance to modish clichés, where the overall impact is more important than any specific meaning the words may have. We assimilate Calzonzín's speech as so much meaningless sloganeering.

As a consequence, the fluctuation between a transparent language and less-than-meaningful jokes is one of the outstanding features of *Los Supermachos*. Of course, what the strip attempts to identify through this type of opaque or meaningless language is the linguistic phenomenon known in Mexico as the *albur*. In the *albur*, two or more persons carry on an apparently harmless conversation. But at bottom it is really charged with double meanings, which in the main are scabrous and scatalogical. The *albur* may be no more than an occasional pastime. But it is clear that it can also serve the more serious goal of fragmenting language practices. It would thus be impossible not to conceive of the *albur* as figuring prominently in popular comic books.

Let us turn now to the sociocultural setting of *Golpe de estado en San Garabato*. We may identify in general terms as its goal the highlighting of a certain "stylish" political process at a given moment in Latin America. It is a process that does not apply directly to Mexico (if it did, the comic book would not be possible), since Mexico has enjoyed over fifty years of institutional continuity. But it is unfortunately a common enough phenomenon, with which Mexicans are familiar through the press, and one that ironically "marginates" modern Mexico precisely because that country has not experienced this idiosyncratic Latin American reality. *Golpe* is from the year 1977, and by that date there had already been a decade of violent political transformations in Latin America whereby an inventory of democratically elected presidents gave way to a cabal of military men promoted to president thanks to a coup d'état. Thus, the coup had become a very real form of political process in Latin America. During the same period and despite the fact that Mexico pursued a course of constitutional government, there was concern in some quarters about the possibility of a move against institutionality by extremists from either the Left or the Right. Thus, this issue of Los Supermachos aligns itself with a political process that in a handful of years had come to constitute a norm.

If the comic speaks of coups as natural phenomena, it nevertheless focuses on them as a political novelty that has yet to reach San Garabato, mired in its backwardness and bent under the yoke of a very traditional feudal bossism. Hence, the coup may be offered as something "progressive," "modern," "desirably up-to-date," or as a redefinition of the structure of power in the village. The value of the coup is touted, as if to say: "We are so backward that we haven't even ever had a coup. Therefore, let's have a coup so we can be just as modern as everyone else."

If the coup provides a golden opportunity for the quick-witted, it is also nothing less than the latest fashion for exploiting the "modernization" of San Garabato. Throughout the Los Supermachos series there are a considerable number of satiric and sardonic references to details of an ideological mythology of progress and modernization: Calzonzín's electrified blanket is more modern than just any old blanket lacking cord and plug. There are countless references to features of this sort, to superficially desirable values, ones that are however framed by the strip with a critical humorism that reveals their false pretenses while demonstrating also why such values are so controversial in Latin America as an imperialistically dictated set of criteria imposed on Mexico by a foreign capitalism and, in turn, by Mexico on San Garabato. This circumstance extends also to the pseudointellectualism of the Left, represented by that opportunistic camp follower, Don Lucas, the pharmacist. It is no accident, in terms of the rhetoric of Los Supermachos, that this pseudoleftist insists on being called by the gentleman's title, don.

There is yet another ironic process that underlies these strips: the constant allusions to the federal capital as the last word as a model for what the entire country should be like. The events that unfold in San Garabato are time and again the pallid, distorted, or exaggerated reflection of the latest style in Mexico City: If they are talking about popular revolutions, fine, let's not be hicks, we'll have our own coup d'état in San Garabato, and we'll do away with the tyranny of the municipal president, Don Perpetuo. For Los Supermachos, the constant series of ironic allusions to the country defined in the exclusive terms of the capital emerges as a sort of denunciation of internal imperialism in a Latin American society where the head shakes the body: The country as a whole is defined in terms of the repetition of the structures and processes of the capital. Thus, the strip postulates a circumstance or situation that is highly ironic in terms of a distinctly desirable goal—that of catching up by having a coup. The irony of this proposition is underscored in the comic by juxtaposing the political process of the coup on the one hand with the phenomenon of the *beata* on the other.

In reality, the structure of the strip is a bit poorly conceived, in the sense that we have a first part that presents a gallery of the usual characters of San Garabato, followed by the encounter between Calzonzín and Doña Eme, only to move on to a series of pages concerning the newspaper article describing the attractive prize for whoever can demonstrate the existence of the human soul. It is only after this encounter that the details of the coup are played out, a coup that becomes possible only when the whole town rushes off after the prize. The element of hypocritical holiness (*beatería*) thus serves to trigger the political pseudorevolution. Although it brings together two of the favorite themes of *Los Supermachos*—*beatería* (see the issue, *Jesucristo en San Garabato*) and the sociopolitical pretentions of modern Mexico—this organization lends rather the impression that, given the extended meeting between Calzonzín and Doña Eme, pages from one issue have gotten mixed up with those from another.

How are these elements brought together in a narrative? The comic sets up a situation in order to comment on it through drawings and dialogs. In the case of *Golpe de estado en San Garabato,* the text rests on the juxtaposition of the two themes of religious hypocrisy and pseudorevolution, such that a false ideal triggers the elaboration of another, equally deceptive one. How are twenty-five or forty pages of a comic fleshed out on this basis is the problem of all narratives: how to make the transition from a narrative kernel to a fully developed text.

In the case of materials like *Los Supermachos,* we need to look at the procedure of narrative development: the elaboration of the essential elements of the plot. As far as comic books are concerned (or soap operas and *fotonovelas,* for that matter), the processes of ecphrasis are, though systematic, not very rigorous, to the extent that they do not require any sort of sophisticated internal logic such as we associate with the serious novel, for example. Often there are intercalated digressions that seem to have little to do with the principal thrust of the strip. But this material is added to achieve the proper text length without seriously detracting from the dominant story line. In the case of a series of comics that make use of the same fictional cast of characters and setting, this can be accomplished by repeating from one issue to another recurring humorous and defining situations relating to the characters' tics and foibles. These running gags are the staples of comic book art.

As a result, the reader of the comic book accepts a certain lack of coherency and density in a text and a certain degree of repetition of situations between numbers. To be sure, this feature facilitates the reading of a comic book because it affirms the identity of the product and of the thematic and narrative constants that underlie it. The encounters between Calzonzín and Doña Eme are one of the constants of *Los Supermachos*, elements that are consequently added to all the issues to round out the number of required pages. The end effect, in any case, is a marginality for these additions that is somewhat parallel (if not contradictory) vis-à-vis the dominant topic of the issue, which is precisely what provides the frequent impression that panels from one strip have gotten mixed in with those of another. Yet, we must also recognize the possibility that, just as in the case of subthemes in high narrative, the digressions may well reinforce or sustain indirectly the central postulate of the strip.

Another typical element to be found in *Golpe* is the doubling of themes that we see in the juxtaposition of the subjects of religious hypocrisy and pseudorevolution. Any incoherency of this juxtaposition is attenuated by the common denominator of the two: Both are false values that exercise a seductive attraction over people. There are also many other details of doubling, whereby the allusion to one event implies identity of another one that is similar in its basic meaning. In general terms, these comic books are a bit like grab bags in that they bring together many disparate topics whose only mutual coherency rests with the fact that they are current topics related to the political and sociocultural values of contemporary Mexico. The controlling focus of the strip brings them together and brings out their similarities by narrativizing them in the fictional world of San Garabato, where the overall phenomenological impression they can give is more important than any strictly internal logical cohesion; all of which leads us back to the distorting and deforming processes in a comic whose basic image is that of a detailed local colorism.

In part, this strategy for dealing with the themes and the mechanism of narrative elaboration leads to a problem of patronizing in *Los Supermachos* (this is especially true after the exit of Rius from Editorial Meridiano). The "author" (in reality, an unidentified team of Meridiano employees) assumes the right to satirize mercilessly values and beliefs that are, to one degree or another, popular, with the clear implication that anyone who subscribes to them must be stupid. Complicity in this belief is invited from the reader of any one of Mexico's social strata. The allies of the author thus have by implication both the right and the duty to mock and repudiate such values by virtue of their presupposed analytical superiority, which legitimatizes the ironic scrutiny of the "simple folk." In this sense, the satirizing of national values cannot help but be also the putting down of aspects of the popular masses. This is a basic problem encountered in liberal critiques and those from the moderate Left, and few authors are able to resolve it adequately. The cast of *Los Supermachos* is not free of the problem, which has contributed to the controversies surrounding the strip. But it should be obvious that, for the readers whose massive purchases of the comic have made it famous, either this is a question to be ignored, or they are willing to overlook it because of the greater interest *Los Supermachos* is able to sustain in its own special brand of humor.

Nevertheless, one of the focuses of the comic in its choice of narrative material is the attempt to define the events, attitudes, speech, opinions, behavior, and such of the people of the village of San Garabato as a sort of microcosm of the Mexican republic. What the reader is therefore called on to grasp, in a "competent" reading of any one of the issues of *Los Supermachos*, is a version in miniature, one that is both costumbristic and expressionistic, of Mexico in its general outlines. One of the goals is to overcome the dichotomy between the vast and teeming capital and the backwater villages of the country that are not supposed to have much to do with the purportedly more advanced and sophisticated life of the metropolis.

Rius and his successors have wanted to bridge the abyss of this situation by showing how the values of the big city get translated into the attempts at sophistication in the villages: The sardonic joke about events in San Garabato is not that they do not live up to the model of the capital, but rather that the San Garabatos of Mexico inexorably translate the model however they may see fit. To imply the sweep of Mexican socioculture on the basis of San Garabato is one of the great feats of the strip that Rius created. Toward carrying out this correlation between San Garabato as the synthesis of Mexico and the capital, *Los Supermachos* wields a series of ironies that are far from subtle and often heavy-handed, like the language of the characters, which merely repeats the rhetoric of the bureaucrats and the ruptures in the pretentious designs of the village sharpies.

Irony is an important process in this type of popular literature, since it functions to correlate appearances and what is maintained as reality in defiance of which such appearances operate. Perception of this ironic play is part of the complicity demanded by an adequate reading of the strip; if the irony comes off as rather obvious, it is to ensure this complicity on the part of the mass reading public the comic has come to count on. As a consequence, the unequivocal denouement of *Golpe de estado en San Garabato*, where the ironic distance between the return to the old, eternal structures and the illusion Don Lucas wishes to sustain so stubbornly could not be more categoric. Don Lucas's words are at variance with what everyone knows to be the case, and the same is true of the commonplaces of revolution he articulates and the exploitation that he wishes to impose at the same time as the "victor" in the game of political power: "Vamos a ver quién lleva la mejor parte."

A major feature of these strips involves an inner point of view that cushions in part the patronizing referred to above. This is so in the sense that, since such a perspective belongs to one of the protagonists, the narrator's scrutinizing eye is transferred in part to the world under examination. This interior duplication belongs to Calzonzín, whose questioning and surprise in the face of what goes on in San Garabato serves to embody the spirit of the strip and to match the ideal stance the reader is invited to assume. Calzonzín is, from inside the strip, the one who is most observant and the one who most criticizes the others, even though he may himself embody some of the false values of his society.

Yet, Calzonzín basically stands apart from the other characters of his setting by virtue of the fact that he is the only one truly capable of commenting on the others and their behavior. Often this commentary is limited to a wordless reaction, as in the many panels where, in the face of the words and deeds of the others, Calzonzín is shown with a startled look on his face and accompanied by a balloon with exclamation points. One must suppose this is how the reader is to react, who is able to follow the sort of social analysis the comic engages in. This is why, too, Calzonzín closes many of the strips with a ringing observation, one that is often sarcastic, that synthesizes the sense of things the strip has undertaken to represent in such detail.

With this sort of strategy, *Los Supermachos* rises above the facile patronizing stemming from the superior optics of the creator-intellectual, ensuring not only the internal validation of its criticism, but also making explicit on the level of the mass reader—who is more likely in background and value code to identify with Calzonzín than with the anonymous artist—the controlling point of view being sought. It is structural strategies like these that have given *Los Supermachos* its extensive and solid success among readers, massive in number and representative of the most diverse sociocultural strata in Mexico.

PLATE 8.1

PLATE 8.1 *continued*

PLATE 8.1 *(continued)*

9

Acevedo and De-Disneyfication

 Although all comparisons are ultimately invidious, it would be impossible to avoid alluding to Walt Disney's Mickey Mouse in order to understand fully the range of meanings that are to be found in Juan Acevedo's clever comic strip, *¡Hola, Cuy!* (Hi, Gopher!). Alluding to the Disney creations gives resonance to the comic strip of the Andean rodent, with Mickey Mouse as both a pretext and a point of departure for Acevedo's graphic narrations and imaginative portrayal of the "Cuy's" characteristics.

What Acevedo proposes is the imperative to transcend and subvert the Disney comic by creating a constellation of autochthonous referents concerning the characters and narration, while concurrently maintaining the referential signs of the North American comic strip. This point could be interpreted as an unfortunate contradiction if it were not for the tension created between the foreign model (generally condescending and debasing in its general parameters, as many critics have pointed out) and the substitute Latin American paradigm. As a part of its internal process, this particularly compensatory relationship not only establishes the suspense of dynamically evoking other possible national value systems but also echoes the ideology of positively displacing current cultural models. Substitution and not supplementation becomes the basis of Acevedo's ideology, since his purpose is not to diffuse a humble regional product as merely another trivial imitation of the cultural dictates of the vias of international consumption, but to metamorphosize the treacherous and dominating icons into referent signs of local values whose merit consists of not competing with, but referring to more global and popular cultural systems and their traditional meaning.

It would be counterproductive to trace the unavoidable parallels that result from the foregoing observations. Any reader of *Cuy* must have been and probably will continue to be, in spite of "knowing better," a consumer not only of the Disney comics but also of the host of similiar graphic artifacts that aggressively innundate the Latin American market. Acevedo's work is noteworthy not so much for *what* he does, but for *how* he has ideologically defined the substitution in terms of replacing the Disney characters with Peruvian counterparts as well as underlying and foregrounding the process by which he carries out this substitution.

An immediately outstanding characteristic of Acevedo's art is the imperative to make his comic strip *personae dramatis* everything that the repressive bourgeois morality of Disney culture prohibits and circumscribes. Therefore, the characters of the Peruvian comic strip assume their natural condition as biological entities (without avoiding the poetic license of finding themselves involved in social situations as well as assimilating the real linguistic codes of their society). For example, the animals of the strip freely exhibit their sexual appendages and/or other primary gender characteristics, in striking contrast to the aggressive asexuality of the world of Disney, where the biological characteristics of male and female are mere conventions and where gender identity is confirmed only by social (a woman's shoes or a man's hat) and not natural/biological conventions. Woven in against the disjunctive semantic backdrop of culture/nature, these categories are reinforced in the behavior of the characters in which being either masculine or feminine is not so much a biological issue but one of imposed social roles. If the manner in which society carries out these impositions is not totally arbitrary, it certainly would appear to be unavoidable.

As a result of these circumstances, a split occurs between the existing power structures that create a hierarchy of values based on sex differences and those other possibilities, seen without the rose-colored glasses of the "charming and funny" Disney conventions, which appear alarmingly abnormal on comparison with existing structures. However, this is a rather complicated issue.

Disney's blatantly masculine world could never be interpreted as a subtle and positive portrait of homosexuality no matter how we perceive the social signs of Mickey Mouse's home, Donald Duck, or a host of other comic strip characters such as Batman or Robin. Once we compare the male-oriented world of North American comics against a possible ideology that recognizes the homosexual experience as just as valid as any other within the framework of human erotic needs, we perceive that comic world as doubly twisted and false: a world that tries to be what it is not and a world that contradicts the facts of social organization.

What is so attractively refreshing in the Peruvian strip is the candor and openness with which sexual and erotic relations are portrayed. This particular facet eloquently deconstructs the repression of sexuality, biological characteristics, and human relations that we find in the impossible fantasy land of Disney's Mickey Mouse. Starting from its frank acceptance of biological characteristics and extending through its treatment of pertinent sociopolitical matters, it goes without saying that Cuy's world challenges its reader to accept it as more "real" and legitimate than the insipid and dehumanized society where Mickey Mouse and his cute little friends live.

This same ideology is to be found in Acevedo's graphic concepts. For over half a century, the Disney studios have been evolving their readily recognizable pyrotechnic style that is the result of the latest and most advanced production methods as well as of the personal organizational hierarchy involved. Acevedo's comic confections are, however, quite "homemade" in their graphic conceptions and in the plot development. Practically all of Disney's comics can be reduced to about half a dozen or so recurring paradigms, if that. Whether in Mickey Mouse or Donald Duck, one group is exploited by the other (children by adults, adults by children, poor by rich, and rich by poor) by such means as blackmail and deception, in such a categorical manner as to be the principal structural leitmotiv of the plots. Acevedo's strips make use of a single plot but metamorphosize it by exploring its derivations and variations throughout the more than one hundred pages of *Cuy*, and in the hundreds of individual corresponding frames. This is a far cry from the narrative simplicity and infantileness that characterize the Disney strips.

The same thing could said about that graphic technique. In Disney's strips, sophisticated technology permits a wide use of color and an assertive imposition of the solid line, all of which are absent in Acevedo's black-and-white creations, which are the indicators of not only economic realities but also metaphoric of regional values in their most primordial and unadorned presentation. The Peruvian strip opts for the bare outline as a less geometric conception that corresponds to a less absolutist interpretation that exercises less control over a prefabricated world. What this means is that, while Disney's artists are unable to waver in their manner of representation because their creations reflect an ethnocentric and rigidly secure view of the world, Acevedo's art deliberately emphasizes the precarious instability of the marginal existence of the Latin American artist, whose only point of reference with exterior models is shown through the skeletal outline of an imported artifact.

This particular aspect of *Cuy* is clearly seen in those segments where the repressive forces, among them certain Disney characters, take over. The aggressive and self-sufficient graphic representations contrast markedly with the very modest norms of the Peruvian product. Without having to discard completely the imperialistic model, Acevedo reconfirms how Disney's comics serve as a countercultural referent that effectively accentuates the authenticity and social pertinence of a comic strip that reflects the important issues facing the Latin American reader.

Cuy's initial naiveness and the progressive perception of what is in fact at stake in important social concerns underlie the cultural productivity of this comic strip in a way that profoundly transcends the "entertainment ideology" at the core of Disney's productions. Besides, Acevedo legitimates his artistic decisions by means of constantly contrasting the validity of "our" experience with the plastic and artificial images that foreign models impose in their place. By stimulating an alternative appreciation and by deconstructing the so-called innocence of imported cultural products, Acevedo's important Peruvian strip promotes a revisionist reading of current dominant cultural codes.

PLATE 9.1

PLATE 9.2

Selected Bibliography

Acevedo, Juan. 1981a. *Para hacer historietas.* Madrid: Popular.

————. 1981b. *¡Hola, Cuy!* Lima: Editora Ital.

Acosta, Mariclaire. 1973. "La historieta cómica en México." *Revista de la Universidad de México* 28, no. 10: 14–19.

Acosta, Raúl. 1974. "Inodoro Pereyra: una historieta argentina." *Crisis* 13: 70–72.

Alemán Sainz, Francisco. 1975. *Las literaturas de kiosco.* Barcelona: Planeta.

Alvarez Constantino, Higilio. 1978. *La magia de los comics coloniza nuestra cultura.* Mexico City.

Amorós, Andrés. 1974. *Subliteraturas.* Barcelona: Ariel.

Barthes, Roland. 1974. *S/Z.* New York: Hill and Wang.

Baur, Elisabeth K. 1978. *La historieta (una experiencia didáctica).* Mexico City: Nueva Imagen.

Borges, Jorge Luis. 1953, 1965. *El "Martín Fierro."* Buenos Aires: Columba.

Borges, Jorge Luis, and Adolfo Bioy Casares. 1955. *Poesia gauchesca.* Mexico City: Fondo de Cultura Económica.

Bourke, John G. 1891. *Scatological Rites of All Nations.* New York: Lowdermilk.

Cañizal, Eduardo Peñuela. 1975. "Quino: uma proposta de leitura." *Vozes* 69, no. 3: 37–48.

Cantón, Dario. 1972. *Gardel, ¿a quién le cantás?* Buenos Aires: Ediciones de la Flor.

Cirne, Moacy. 1973. *A linguagem dos quadrinhos; o universo estrutural de Ziraldo e Mauricio de Sousa.* 3rd ed. Petrópolis: Vozes.

Clinton, Stephen T. 1978. "Censorship, Human Rights Under Videla." *Latin American Digest* 12, no. 2: 1–2.

Cultura y dependencia; ocho ensayos latinoamericanos. 1975. Caracas: Monte Avila.

Dijk, Teun Adrianus van. 1980. *Text and Context: Explorations in the Semantics and Pragmatics of Discourse*. London and New York: Longman.

Donni de Mirande, Nélida. 1967. *La lengua coloquial y la lengua de la literatura argentina*. Rosario: Universidad Nacional del Litoral, Cuadernos del Instituto de Letras.

Dorfles, Gillo. 1969a. *Kitsch, the World of Bad Taste*. New York: Bell.

———. 1969b. *Nuevos ritos nuevos mitos*. Barcelona: Lumen.

Dorfman, Ariel. 1983. *The Empire's Old Clothes: What the Lone Ranger, Babar, and Other Innocent Heroes Do to Our Minds*. New York: Pantheon Books.

Dorfman, Ariel, and Manuel Joffré. 1974. *Supermán y sus amigos del alma*. Buenos Aires: Galerna.

Dorfman, Ariel, and Armand Mittelart. 1972. *Para leer al Pato Donald*. Buenos Aires: Siglo Veintiuno Argentina.

Eco, Umberto. 1974. "Mafalda la disconforme." In Joaquín Salvador Lavado, *Mafalda; y digo yo . . . .* Barcelona: Noveno Arte.

———. 1977. *Apocalípticos e integrados*. 5th ed. Barcelona: Lumen.

Eisler, Ken. 1967. "Mexico's New Race: 'Los Supermachos.'" *Texas Quarterly* 10, no. 4: 182–197.

Fernández Aguilar, Javier. 1969. "Rius." *Presagio; pensamiento y acción de la juventud* 11: 32–33.

Ferrer, Arturo Horacio. 1970. *El libro del tango; historias e imágenes*. Buenos Aires: Editorial Ossorio-Vargas.

Fontanarrosa, Roberto. 1973. *Quién es Fontanarrosa*. Buenos Aires: Ediciones de la Flor.

———. 1974– . *Boogie, el aceitoso*. Buenos Aires: Ediciones de la Flor; *Proceso, seminario de información y análisis en México*.

———. 1974. *Las aventuras de Inodoro Pereyra ¡El Renegau! Poema telúrico de Fontanarrosa*. Buenos Aires: Ediciones de la Flor.

Fossati, Franco. 1980[?]. *Il fumetto argentino*. Genoa: Pirella.

Foster, David William. 1983–1984. "Narrative Rights in the Argentine Tango." *Symposium* 37: 261–271.

———. 1984. "Recent Works on Latin American Cartoon Art." *Studies in Latin American Popular Culture* 3: 179–182.

———. 1986. "Verdad y ficción en una fotonovela mexicana: la duplicidad genera el texto." *Confluencia; revista hispánica de cultura y literatura* 2, no. 2: 50–59.

Fresnault Dreruelle, Pierre. 1974. "Diseños y globos. La historieta como medio de expresión: el montage." *C línea; revista latinoamericana de estudio de la historieta* 12: 38–45.

Gasca, Luis. 1976. "Los supermachos." In *The World Encyclopedia of Comics*, ed. Maurice Horn. New York: Chelsea House, p. 642. See also the entry on *Los agachados*, p. 68.

Golpe de estado en San Garabato. 1977. *Los Supermachos* 575. Mexico City: Editorial Meridiano.

Grassi, A. 1971. *¿Qué es la historieta?* Buenos Aires: Columba.

Greenblatt, Stephen. 1979. "Filthy Rites." *University Publishing* 8: 5–6.

Greimas, Algirdas Julien. 1971. *Semántica estructural, investigación metodológica*. Madrid: Gredos.

Greimas, Algirdas Julien, and Joseph Courtès. 1982. *Semiotics and Language: An Analytic Dictionary*. Bloomington: Indiana University Press.

Gubern, Román. 1972. *El lenguaje de los comics*. Barcelona: Peninsula.

Güiraldes, Ricardo. 1926. *Don Segundo Sombra*. Buenos Aires: Editorial Proa.

Hernández, José. 1872. *El gaucho Martín Fierro*. Buenos Aires: Imprenta de la Pampa. Innumerable subsequent editions.

———. 1879. *La vuelta de Martín Fierro*. Buenos Aires: Librería del Plata. Innumerable subsequent editions. This entry and former usually published together under title *Martín Fierro*.

Hernandez, Pablo José. 1975. *Para leer a Mafalda*. Buenos Aires: Ediciones Meridiano.

Herner, Irene. 1979. *Mitos y monitos; historietas y fotonovelas en México*. Mexico City: Universidad Nacional Autónoma de México/Nueva Imagen.

Hesse, Thomas B., and John Ashbury, eds. 1970. *Narrative Art*. New York: Macmillan.

Hinds, Harold E., Jr. 1977. "'No hay fuerza más poderosa que la mente humana'—Kalimán." *Hispamérica* 18: 31–46.

———. 1979. "Algunas reflexiones sobre la historieta mexicana." *Artes visuales* 22: 30–31.

———. 1982. *"El Payo*: una solución popular a la lucha mexicana entre los robatierras y los descamisados." *Hispamérica* 31: 33–49.

"La historieta mexicana." 1972. *Artes de México* 158: 1–91.

Hodge, Robert. 1976. "Linguistics and Popular Culture." In *Approaches to Popular Cultures*, ed. C. W. E. Bigsby. Bowling Green, OH: Bowling Green University Popular Press.

Horn, Maurice. 1976. *World Encyclopedia of Comics*. New York: Chelsea House.

Jameson, Fredric. 1981. *The Political Unconscious: Narrative as a Socially Symbolic Act*. Ithaca, NY: Cornell University Press.

Jitrik, Noé. 1971. "El tema del canto en el *Martín Fierro*, de José Hernández." In his *El fuego de la especie; ensayos sobre seis escritores argentinos*. Buenos Aires: Siglo XXI Argentina.

Kempkes, Wolfgang. 1974. *International Bibliography of Comics Literature*. New York: R. R. Bowker.

Koch, Dolores. 1981. *"Mafalda*: recursos narrativos de la tira cómica." In *Literature and Popular Culture in the Hispanic World: A Symposium*, ed. Rose S. Minc. Gaithersberg, MD: Hispamérica; Upper Montclair, NJ: Montclair State College.

Kress, G. R. 1976. "Structuralism and Popular Culture." In *Approaches to Popular Culture*, ed. C. W. E. Bigsby. Bowling Green, OH: Bowling

Green University Popular Press.

Lindstrom, Naomi. 1980. "Social Commentary in Argentine Cartooning: From Description to Questioning." *Journal of Popular Culture* 14, no. 3: 509–523.

Lucie-Smith, Edward. 1981. *The Art of Caricature*. Ithaca, NY: Cornell University Press.

Lugones, Leopoldo. 1916. *El payador*. Buenos Aires: Centurión.

"Mafalda Hopes the World Solves Its Problems." 1976. *Maryknoll Magazine* (December): 34–36.

"Mafalda: la niña cumple 17 años y está muy fuerte." 1981. *Superhumor* 9: 47–52.

Mafud, Julio. 1966. *Sociología del tango*. Buenos Aires: Américalee.

———. 1973. *Los argentinos y el status*. 6a ed. Buenos Aires: Editorial Américalee.

———. 1973. *Psicología de la viveza criolla; contribuciones para una interpretación de la realidad social argentina y americana*. 5a ed. Buenos Aires: Editorial Américalee.

———. 1976. *La viveza criolla, los argentinos y el status:* Buenos Aires.

Masiello, Francine R. 1978. "Jail House Flicks: Projections by Manuel Puig." *Symposium* 32: 15–24.

Masotta, Oscar. 1968. "Reflexiones presiomológicas sobre la historieta: el 'esquematismo'." In his *Conciencia y estructura*. Buenos Aires: Jorge Alvarez.

———. 1970. *La historieta en el mundo moderno*. Buenos Aires: Paidós.

Medina, Enrique. 1976. *Strip-tease*. Buenos Aires: Editorial Corredigor.

———. 1977. *Perros de la noche*. Buenos Aires: Editorial Eskol.

Méndez, José Luis. 1975. "Manipulación y fabricación de mitos en la subliteratura." *Casa de las Américas* 89: 122–129.

Meson, Danusia L. 1981. "Mafalda y la crítica pura (?) de la razon y el orden." In *Literature and Popular Culture in the Hispanic World: A Symposium*, ed. Rose S. Minc. Gaithersburg, MD: Hispamérica; Upper Montclair, NJ: Montclair State College.

Mira, J. Eduardo. 1971. "Notes on a Comparative Analysis of American and Spanish Comic Books." *Journal of Popular Culture* 5, no. 1: 203–222.

Miranda, Orlando. 1976. *Tio Patinhas e os mitos da comunicação*. São Paulo: Summus.

Moffatt, Alfredo. 1967. *Estrategias para sobrevivir en Buenos Aires:* Buenos Aires.

Moix, Ana Maria. 1973. *24 x 24 (entrevistas)*. Barcelona: Peninsula.

Monsiváis, Carlos. 1978. "Notas sobre cultura popular en México." *Latin American Perspectives* 5, no. 1: 98–118.

Moorehead, Alan. 1969. *Darwin and the Beagle*. New York: Harper and Row.

Morales, Fidel. 1974. "La historieta pide definirse." *C línea; revista latinoamericana de estudio de la historieta* 6: 6–11.

Muraro, Heriberto J. 1974. "Poner el caballo delante del carro: la estatización de la TV argentina." *Crisis* 16: 8–13.

Naipaul, V. S. 1980. *The Return of Eva Peron, with the Killings in Trinidad.* New York: Alfred A. Knopf.

Nomez, Naim. 1974. "La historieta en el proceso de cambio social." *Comunicación y cultura* 2: 109–123.

Parent, Georges-A. 1982. "Focalization: A Narratological Approach to Mexican Illustrated Stories." *Studies in Latin American Popular Culture* 1: 201–212.

Poniatowska, Elena. 1968. "Rius, ese seminarista." *Siempre* 800: 40–41, 69–70.

Proctor, Phyllis A. 1973. *Mexico's Supermachos: Satire and Social Revolution in Comics by Rius.* Dissertation Abstracts International 33: 5138A.

Propp, Vladimir. 1968. *The Morphology of the Folk Tale.* Austin: University of Texas Press.

Las puertitas del Sr. López. 1980. Text by Carlos Trillo; drawings by Horacio Altuna. Introduction by Juan Sasturain. Buenos Aires: Ediciones de la Urraca.

Puig, Manuel. 1968. *La traición de Rita Hayworth.* Buenos Aires: Editorial J. Alvarez.

———. 1976. *El beso de la mujer araña.* Barcelona: Editorial Seix Barral.

Pratt, Mary Louise. 1977. *Toward a Speech Act Theory of Literary Discourse.* Bloomington: Indiana University Press.

Quino [Lavado, Joaquín Salvador]. 1967–1974. *Mafalda.* Buenos Aires: Ediciones de la Flor.

———. 1977. *Mafalda.* Mexico City: Nueva Imagen.

"Quino." [1972]. *Informaciones argentinas* 49: 47.

Río, Eduardo del (Rius). 1972. *La caricatura mexicana. Los agachados.* 104: complete issue.

Rivera, Jorge B. 1976a. "'. . . una compadrada contra el terror': historia del humor gráfico argentino (II)." *Crisis* 35: 57–63.

———. 1976b. "¡Sonaste, maneco! Historia del humor gráfico argentino I." *Crisis* 34: 16–24.

Rodríguez Diéguez, José Luis. 1977. "El cómic como instrumento de enseñanza." In *Las funciones de la imagen en la enseñanza.* Barcelona: Gustavo Gili.

Roffé, Reina. 1976. *Monte de Venus.* Buenos Aires: Editorial Corregidor.

Sábat, Hermenegildo. 1971. *Al troesma con cariño.* Buenos Aires: Siglo Veintiuno Argentina.

———. 1972. *Yo Bix, tú Bix, él Bix (I Bix, you Bix, he Bix).* Buenos Aires: Editorial Airene.

———. 1974. *Georgie dear.* Buenos Aires: Editorial Crisis.

———. 1975. *Seré breve; una selección de dibujos publicados entre los años 1971 y 1975.* [Buenos Aires?]: Editorial La Garza.

———. 1979. *Dogor; diez láminas.* Buenos Aires: Sociedad de Distribuidor de Diarios, Revista y Afines.

————. 1980. *Monsieur Lautrec*. Madrid: Ameris.

"Scat, la realidad de un sueño recurrente." 1975. *Crisis* 21: 70.

Sempere, Pedro. 1976. *Semiología del infortunio; lenguaje e ideología de la fotonovela*. Madrid: Felmar.

Serafini, Horacio, and Roberto Bardin. 1976. "La inocencia de la historieta." *Cambio* 49–53.

Smith, Barbara Herrnstein. 1978. *On the Margins of Discourse: The Relation of Literature to Language*. Chicago: University of Chicago Press.

Sotres, M. Bertha Eugenia. 1973. "La cultura de los comics." *Revista mexicana de ciencia política* 74: 13–18.

Speck, Paula M. 1982. "Rius for Beginners: A Study in Comicbook Satire." *Studies in Latin American Popular Culture* 1: 113–124.

Steimberg, Oscar. 1971. "El lugar de Mafalda." *Los libros* 17: 6–7.

————. 1977. *Leyendo historietas; estilos y sentidos de un "arte menor."* Buenos Aires: Nueva Visión.

Los Supermachos. 1967. *México/This Month* 13, no. 5: 26–28.

Tatum, Charles, and Harold Hinds. 1979. "Eduardo del Río (Rius): An Interview and Introductory Essay." *Chasqui* 9, no. 1: 3–23.

Todorov, Tzvetan. 1969. *Grammaire du Décaméron*. The Hague: Mouton.

————. 1971. *Poétique de la prose*. Paris: Seuil.

Trillo, Carlos, and Guillermo Saccomanno. 1981. *Historia de la historieta argentina*. Buenos Aires: Record.

Tubau, Ivan. 1971. *Dibujando historietas*. Barcelona: Ceac.

Vázquez Lucio, Oscar E. (Siulnas). 1985. *Historia del humor gráfico y escrito en la Argentina*. Buenos Aires: Editorial Universitaria de Buenos Aires.

Vega, Pastor. 1974. "Pequeña crítica ideológica de los llamados cómics en América latina." *Cine cubano* 81–83: 1–11.

Verbitsky, Bernardo. 1957. *Villa miseria también es América*. Buenos Aires: G. Kraft.

Villariño, Idea. 1977. "El tango cantado." *Texto crítico* 6: 37–48.

Zuna, José Guadalupe. 1961. *Historia de la caricatura en México*. Guadalajara: Universidad de Guadalajara.

Index

About the Book
and the Author

Professor Foster examines major examples of graphic humor in Latin America, and especially in Argentina and Mexico, focusing exclusively on those materials that make use of the modes and formula of mass art to reflect critically on social and cultural ideologies. This kind of humor, although part of the commercial distribution of culture, serves both to refute the conformist ideology of mass art and to stimulate in those that read it a deconstructionist attitude toward that ideology in the name of heightened social consciousness and cultural self-reflection. Foster covers graphic humor ranging from the drawings of the Mexican Rius, to such major Argentine figures as Quino, Hermenegildo Sábat (of Uruguayan origin), and Roberto Fontanarrosa, to work by the Brazilian Ziraldo and the Peruvian Juan Acevedo. He is particularly concerned with providing in tandem a content analysis of the drawings and analysis of the artistic strategies employed in the process of graphically depicting content.

David William Foster is professor of Spanish at Arizona State University, where he also directs the publication program of the university's Center for Latin American Studies.